i

This book focuses on Google Drive and gives you clear, helpful information to make it easier to understand.

Whether you're just starting out or have some experience with tech, this book is here to guide you. I hope it helps you feel more confident, sparks your creativity, and makes mastering Google Drive simple and fun.

Table of Contents

Introduction 2

   1. What is Google Drive? 2

     Overview of Cloud Storage 2

     Benefits of Using Google Drive 3

     Who Is This Guide For? 4

   2. Getting Started with Google Drive 4

     Creating a Google Account 4

     Accessing Google Drive on Different Platforms 8

     Understanding Google Drive's Free vs. Paid Storage Plans 10

     Choosing the Right Plan: 11

Chapter 1: Navigating the Google Drive Interface 13

   1. Web Interface Overview 13

     Menu Bar and Navigation Pane 13

     File List and Grid View 14

     Search Bar and Filters 15

   2. Desktop Interface Overview 16

     Installing and Setting Up the Desktop App 16

     Syncing Local Folders with Google Drive 17

   3. Mobile App Overview 18

     Exploring the Mobile App Layout 18

     Mobile-Specific Features 19

Chapter 2: Managing Files and Folders 20

1. Uploading Files and Folders 20

   Drag-and-Drop Method 20

   Uploading Through the Menu 21

2. Creating Folders 24

   Organizing Files into Folders 24

   Renaming, Moving, and Deleting Folders 25

3. Using Colors and Labels 26

   Assigning Colors to Folders for Easy Identification 26

   Using the "Starred" Feature for Important Files 27

Chapter 3: Creating and Editing Files 29

1. Introduction to Google Workspace Apps 29

   Overview of Google Docs, Sheets, Slides, and Forms 29

2. Creating New Files 30

   Starting a Blank Document or Using Templates 30

   Saving Files in Different Formats (PDF, Word, etc.) 33

3. Basic Editing Tips 33

   Adding Text, Images, and Tables 34

   Formatting Options and Shortcuts 35

Chapter 4: File Sharing and Permissions 36

1. Sharing Files and Folders 36

   Sending Files via Links 36

   Sharing through Email Invitations 38

2. Permission Levels 39

Viewer, Commenter, and Editor Roles.. 39

Managing Permissions for Multiple Users 40

3. Best Practices for Sharing.. 41

Sharing Securely and Avoiding Unauthorized Access 41

Chapter 5: Collaboration Tools.. 44

1. Real-Time Collaboration.. 44

Working on Files Simultaneously with Others 44

Commenting, Suggesting, and Resolving Changes................................ 45

2. Version History... 48

Viewing and Restoring Previous Versions of a File 48

3. Using Notifications 49

Enabling Notifications for File Updates.. 50

Chapter 6: Searching and Organizing Files......................... 54

1. Using the Search Bar 54

Advanced Search Options 54

Filtering Files by Type, Owner, or Date 57

2. Organizing Files 58

Grouping Files into Folders 58

Using Tags or Descriptions 60

3. Archiving and Deleting Files 64

Moving Files to Trash 64

Recovering Deleted Files 65

Chapter 7: Syncing and Offline Access 67

1. Setting Up Syncing... 67

Configuring the Desktop App 67

Syncing Specific Folders Only 68

2. Accessing Files Offline 69

Enabling Offline Mode.. 69

Editing Files Without an Internet Connection........................ 70

3. Troubleshooting Sync Issues 71

Common Errors and Solutions 71

Chapter 8: Integrating with Google Services............................ **73**

1. Using Google Drive with Gmail..................................... 73

Attaching Drive Files to Emails 73

Saving Email Attachments Directly to Drive......................... 75

2. Google Photos Integration 75

Backing Up Photos to Drive.. 76

3. Integrating with Calendar and Keep................................ 77

Linking Drive Files to Calendar Events............................... 77

Using Keep for Notes and File References 78

Chapter 9: Advanced Features.. **80**

1. Shared Drives... 80

What are Shared Drives?.. 80

Setting Up and Managing a Shared Drive 81

2. File Versions 84

Checking and Restoring File Versions................................ 84

Version Control Best Practices: 85

3. Using Add-ons 85

Enhancing Drive Functionality with Third-Party Tools 85

Chapter 10: Security and Privacy 88

1. File Privacy Settings 88

Controlling Who Can View, Edit, or Share Files 88

2. Account Security 90

Enabling Two-Factor Authentication (2FA) 90

Managing Connected Apps and Devices 93

3. Tips for Secure Sharing 94

Protecting Sensitive Data with Advanced Settings 94

Chapter 11: Google Drive for Mobile 96

1. Overview of the Mobile App 96

Key Differences from the Desktop Version 96

2. Scanning Documents 97

Using Your Phone's Camera to Scan and Upload 97

3. Mobile-Specific Features 98

Using Offline Mode 98

Sharing on the Go 99

Chapter 12: Integrations with Third-Party Apps 101

1. Google Workspace Marketplace 101

Installing and Managing Apps 101

2. Integration with Microsoft Office 103

Editing Word and Excel Files in Drive 103

3. Automating Workflows 104

Using Tools Like Zapier to Automate Repetitive Tasks 104

Chapter 13: Troubleshooting Common Issues 107

1. Storage Management... 107

Freeing Up Space in Drive 107

Identifying and Removing Large Files................................ 108

2. Sync Errors.. 108

Resolving Syncing Problems on Desktop and Mobile 109

3. File Upload Problems 110

Solutions for Failed or Incomplete Uploads...................... 111

Chapter 14: Tips and Tricks for Beginners 113

1. Keyboard Shortcuts 113

Popular Shortcuts to Boost Productivity............................ 113

2. Productivity Tips.. 114

Using Drive for Project Management................................. 114

Setting Up Daily Workflows with Drive 115

3. Creative Uses of Google Drive.. 116

Using Drive for Journaling, Budgeting, and Organizing Personal Files 117

Chapter 15: Best Practices and Conclusion 119

1. Top 10 Tips for Mastering Google Drive............................ 119

2. Encouragement for Exploring Advanced Features.............. 121

3. FAQs 122

Appendices 124

Glossary of Terms... 124

Quick Reference Guide... 125

Google Drive Tips 127

Index **128**

Introduction

1. What is Google Drive?

Overview of Cloud Storage

Cloud storage refers to storing your files on the internet instead of on your computer or mobile device. With cloud storage, your files are securely saved on servers managed by companies like Google. This allows you to:

- Access files from anywhere with an internet connection.
- Sync files across multiple devices.
- Protect files from being lost due to hardware failure.

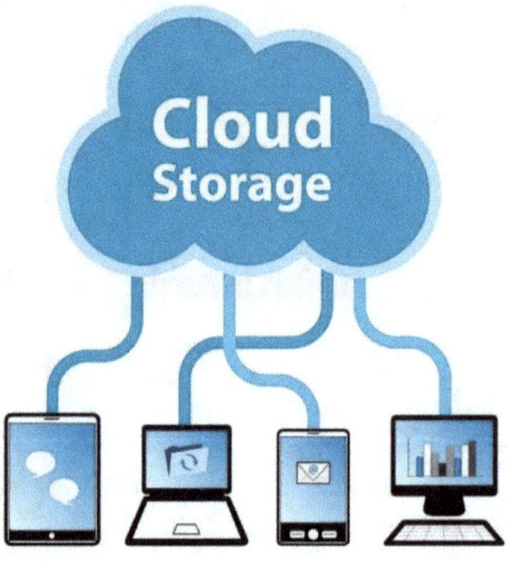

Google Drive is Google's cloud storage platform that not only stores your files but also integrates seamlessly with Google's suite of productivity tools, such as Google Docs, Sheets, and Slides.

Benefits of Using Google Drive

Personal Use:

1. **Anywhere Access:** Whether you're on your computer, smartphone, or tablet, you can access your files anytime, anywhere.
2. **Automatic Syncing:** Upload or edit a file on one device, and it's instantly updated on all devices connected to your account.
3. **Sharing Made Easy:** Share photos, documents, or videos with friends and family in just a few clicks.
4. **Backup and Recovery:** Never lose files due to device damage. Google Drive automatically backs up your data.

Professional Use:

1. **Real-Time Collaboration:** Work with team members simultaneously on the same document or project.
2. **Centralized Storage:** Keep all work-related files in one secure location, easily accessible by your team.
3. **Integration with Productivity Tools:** Use tools like Google Docs and Sheets directly within Drive, avoiding the need for separate applications.
4. **Security and Permissions:** Assign specific roles (viewer, commenter, editor) to collaborators for better control.

Who Is This Guide For?

This guide is designed for:

- **Absolute Beginners:** Those who have never used Google Drive before.
- **Intermediate Users:** People who know the basics but want to explore advanced features like file sharing, syncing, and integrations.
- **Professionals and Students:** Those looking to boost productivity by organizing, collaborating, and managing files efficiently.
- **Curious Learners:** Anyone eager to unlock the full potential of Google Drive for personal or professional tasks.

2. Getting Started with Google Drive

Creating a Google Account

Before you can use Google Drive, you'll need a Google account. Follow these steps:

1. **Go to Google's Homepage**:
   - Open your web browser and visit www.google.com.
2. **Click "Sign In" or "Create Account"**:
   - If you don't already have a Google account, click "Create account" and select "For myself" or "For my child" (if creating for family use).

   Alternatively, just go to accounts.google.com on your web browser.

Sign in

with your Google Account

Email or phone

Forgot email?

Not your computer? Use Guest mode to sign in privately.
Learn more

Create account

Next

3. **Fill in Your Information**:
   o Enter your **first and last name**.
   o Create a **username** (this will also serve as your Gmail address).
   o Set a strong **password** and confirm it.

Create your Google Account

First name | Last name

Username | @gmail.com

You can use letters, numbers & periods

Use my current email address instead

Password | Confirm

Use 8 or more characters with a mix of letters, numbers & symbols

One account. All of Google working for you.

Sign in instead | Next

4. **Provide Additional Information**:
   - Enter your **phone number** and a recovery email (optional, but useful for security and account recovery).
   - Enter your **date of birth** and **gender**.

Create your Google Account

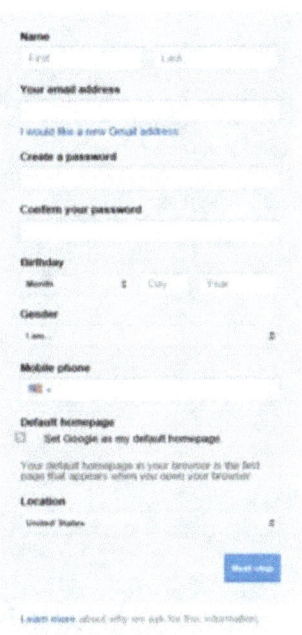

5. **Agree to Terms and Conditions**:
   - Review Google's terms and conditions, then click "I agree."
6. **Verify Your Account**:
   - Google may ask for a phone number verification. Enter the code sent to your mobile device.

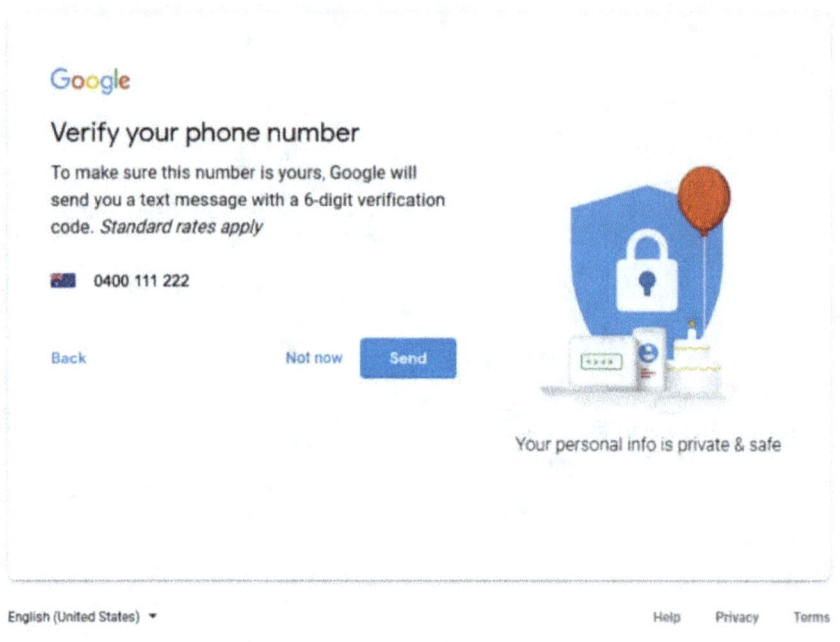

Once your account is created, you're ready to start using Google Drive.

Accessing Google Drive on Different Platforms

1. On a Web Browser:

- Visit drive.google.com and log in using your Google account credentials.
- You'll see the main interface, which includes:
  - **Sidebar**: Quick access to My Drive, Shared with Me, Recent, and Trash.
  - **Main Workspace**: Displays your files and folders.
  - **Search Bar**: Quickly find files using keywords.

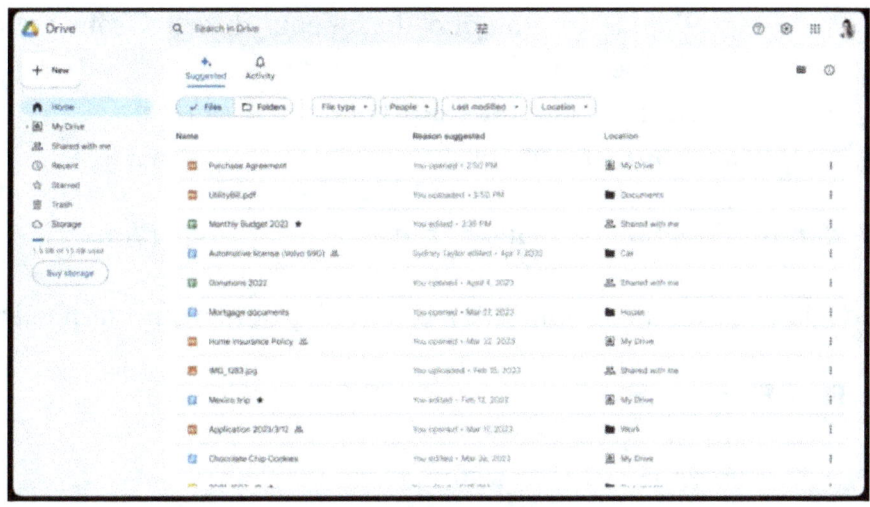

2. On Desktop (Windows or macOS):

- Download and install **Google Drive for Desktop**:
    - o Visit Google Drive for Desktop.
    - o Download the app and follow the installation instructions.
- Set up folder syncing:
    - o Select folders on your computer to sync with Google Drive.
    - o Changes made locally will reflect in Drive, and vice versa.

3. On Mobile (iOS or Android):

- Download the **Google Drive app** from the App Store (iOS) or Google Play Store (Android).
- Log in with your Google account.
- Key features of the mobile app:

- o Upload photos and documents directly from your phone.
- o Scan documents using your phone's camera.
- o Share files on the go.

Understanding Google Drive's Free vs. Paid Storage Plans

Google Drive offers flexible storage plans depending on your needs:

1. Free Plan:

- Includes **15 GB** of free storage.
- Shared across Google Drive, Gmail, and Google Photos.

2. Paid Plans (Google One):

- Starts at **100 GB** for $1.99/month (or $19.99/year).
- Higher tiers include 200 GB, 2 TB, and more.
- Benefits of paid plans:
    - o Extra storage space.
    - o Access to Google experts.
    - o Option to share your storage with family (up to 5 members).

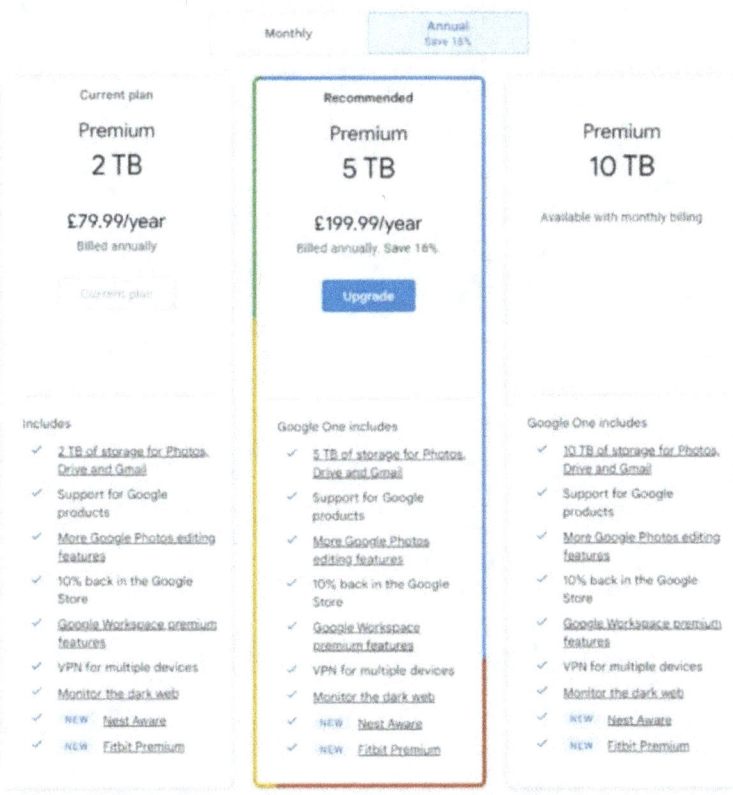

Choosing the Right Plan:

- **Free Plan**: Suitable for light users who only need storage for a small number of documents and photos.
- **100 GB or 200 GB Plan**: Ideal for students or professionals with moderate storage needs.
- **2 TB or Higher Plan**: Best for businesses, photographers, and anyone storing large files or videos.

Chapter 1: Navigating the Google Drive Interface

1. Web Interface Overview

Google Drive's web interface is intuitive and user-friendly. Here's a step-by-step guide to understanding its components:

Menu Bar and Navigation Pane

1. **Access the Web Interface**:
   - Open your browser and visit drive.google.com.
   - Log in with your Google account credentials.
2. **Menu Bar**:
   - Located at the top of the page, it includes:
     - **New Button**: Click to create new files or folders, or upload existing ones.
     - **Settings Gear Icon**: Access Drive settings, such as language, offline mode, and storage usage.
     - **Help Icon**: Access tutorials, troubleshooting tips, or send feedback to Google.
3. **Navigation Pane**:
   - Found on the left-hand side, it includes:
     - **My Drive**: Displays all your files and folders.
     - **Shared with Me**: Shows files and folders shared by others.
     - **Recent**: Lists files you've recently accessed.

- **Starred**: Displays files and folders you've marked as important.
- **Trash**: Contains deleted files for up to 30 days before permanent removal.

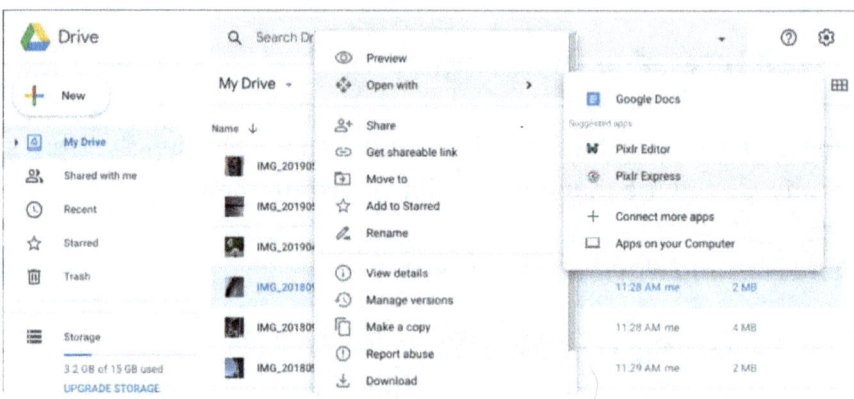

File List and Grid View

1. **File List View**:
   - Files are displayed in a vertical list with details such as file name, owner, last modified date, and size.
   - Click the column headers (e.g., "Name," "Last Modified") to sort files accordingly.
2. **Grid View**:
   - Switch to grid view by clicking the grid icon in the top-right corner.
   - Files and folders are displayed as large, visually distinct thumbnails.

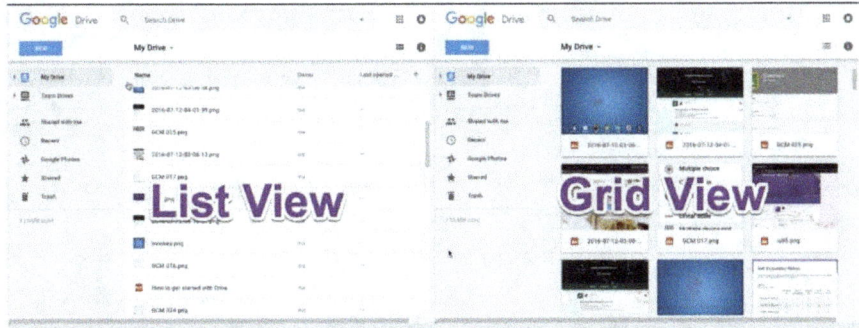

3. **File Options**:
   - Right-click on any file or folder to access options like:
     - **Open with**: Choose an app to open the file.
     - **Share**: Adjust sharing permissions or copy the sharing link.
     - **Move to**: Organize the file into a folder.
     - **Download**: Save a copy to your computer.

Search Bar and Filters

1. **Search Bar**:
   - Located at the top of the page, the search bar allows you to find files quickly by entering keywords or phrases.
2. **Search Filters**:
   - Click the dropdown arrow in the search bar to access filters.
   - Filter by file type (e.g., PDFs, images, videos), owner, or last modified date.

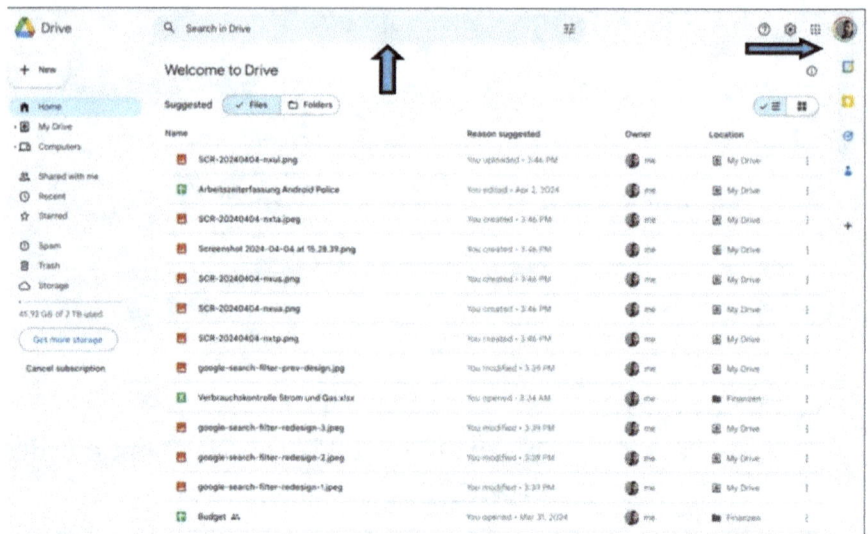

2. Desktop Interface Overview

Google Drive's desktop app simplifies file syncing and offline access. Here's how to navigate it:

Installing and Setting Up the Desktop App

1. **Download the App**:
   o Visit the Google Drive for Desktop page.
   o Download the app for your operating system (Windows or macOS).
2. **Install the App**:
   o Follow the on-screen installation instructions.
   o Open the app once the installation is complete.
3. **Sign In**:
   o Log in using your Google account credentials.

o   Grant necessary permissions to allow the app to access files on your computer.

Google Drive

Syncing Local Folders with Google Drive

1. **Select Folders to Sync**:
   o   Open the app's settings.
   o   Choose the local folders you want to sync with Google Drive.
2. **Two-Way Syncing**:
   o   Any changes made to these folders on your computer will automatically update in Google Drive and vice versa.
3. **Accessing Synced Files**:

o   On your computer, synced files can be found in a folder named **Google Drive** (created during setup).

o   Files can be opened and edited directly from this folder.

4. **Pause or Stop Syncing**:

o   To temporarily stop syncing, click the app icon in the system tray (Windows) or menu bar (macOS) and select **Pause Syncing**.

o   To stop syncing completely, remove the folder from the app's settings.

3. Mobile App Overview

The Google Drive mobile app is optimized for on-the-go file access and management. Here's how to navigate its layout:

Exploring the Mobile App Layout

1. **Download the App**:

o   For Android: Visit the Google Play Store.

o   For iOS: Visit the App Store.

o   Install and log in using your Google account.

2. **Main Dashboard**:

o   The homepage displays recently accessed files for quick access.

3. **Bottom Navigation Bar**:

o   **Home**: Shows recent files and suggestions.

o   **Starred**: Lists important files you've marked as favorites.

o   **Shared**: Displays files shared by or with you.

o   **Files**: Provides a folder-based view of your Drive.

4. **Menu Options**:
   - Access additional features by tapping the hamburger menu (three horizontal lines) in the top-left corner.
   - Options include **Settings**, **Trash**, and account switching.

Mobile-Specific Features

1. **Uploading Files**:
   - Tap the **+ (plus)** button at the bottom-right corner.
   - Choose to upload photos, videos, or other documents from your phone.
2. **Scanning Documents**:
   - Use your phone's camera to scan physical documents.
   - The app automatically converts scans to PDF format for easy storage.
3. **Offline Access**:
   - Mark files as available offline by tapping the three-dot menu next to a file and selecting **Make Available Offline**.
4. **File Sharing**:
   - Share files directly from the app by tapping the three-dot menu next to a file and choosing **Share**.
   - Adjust permissions (Viewer, Commenter, Editor) as needed.

Chapter 2: Managing Files and Folders

1. Uploading Files and Folders

Google Drive makes it easy to upload files and folders from your computer to the cloud. Let's explore the methods:

Drag-and-Drop Method

1. **Access Google Drive**:
   - Open your browser and navigate to drive.google.com.
   - Log in with your Google account.
2. **Locate Files/Folders on Your Computer**:
   - Open the folder on your computer where the file(s) or folder(s) you want to upload are stored.
3. **Drag and Drop**:
   - Select the desired file(s) or folder(s).
   - Drag them into the Google Drive browser window.
   - Release the mouse button to drop them into the desired location within Drive.
   - Wait for the upload progress indicator to confirm the upload is complete.

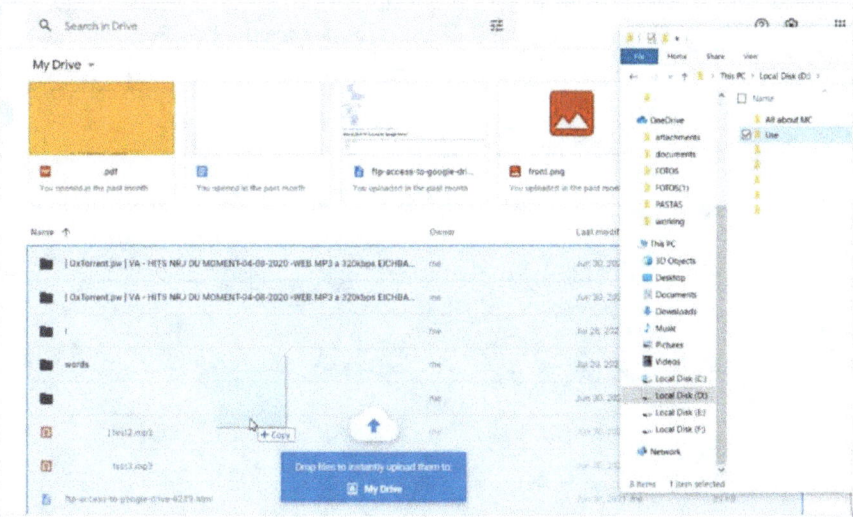

Drag and Drop Files from PC to Google Drive

Uploading Through the Menu

1. **Open the New Menu**:
   - In Google Drive, click the **+ New** button in the top-left corner.

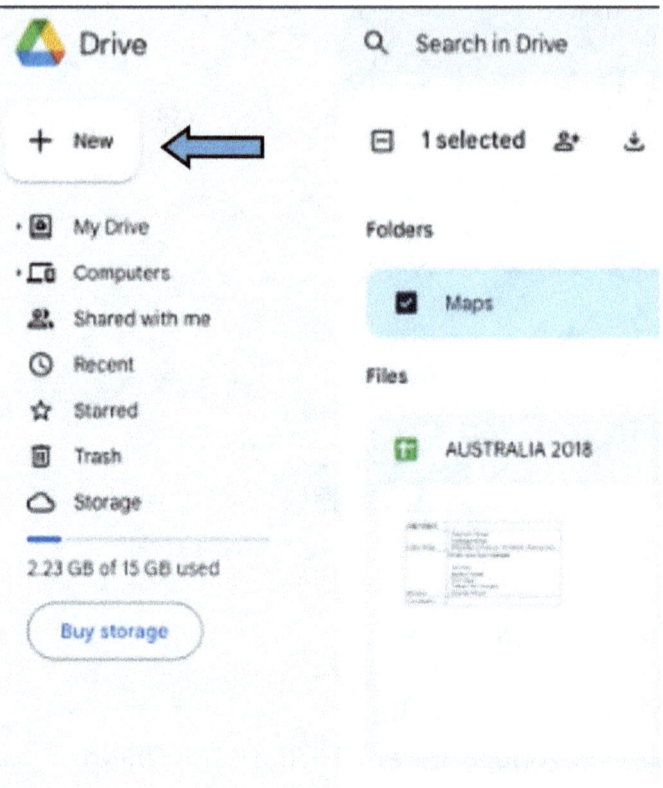

2. **Choose Upload Options**:
   - To upload individual files: Select **File Upload** and browse your computer to choose the file(s).

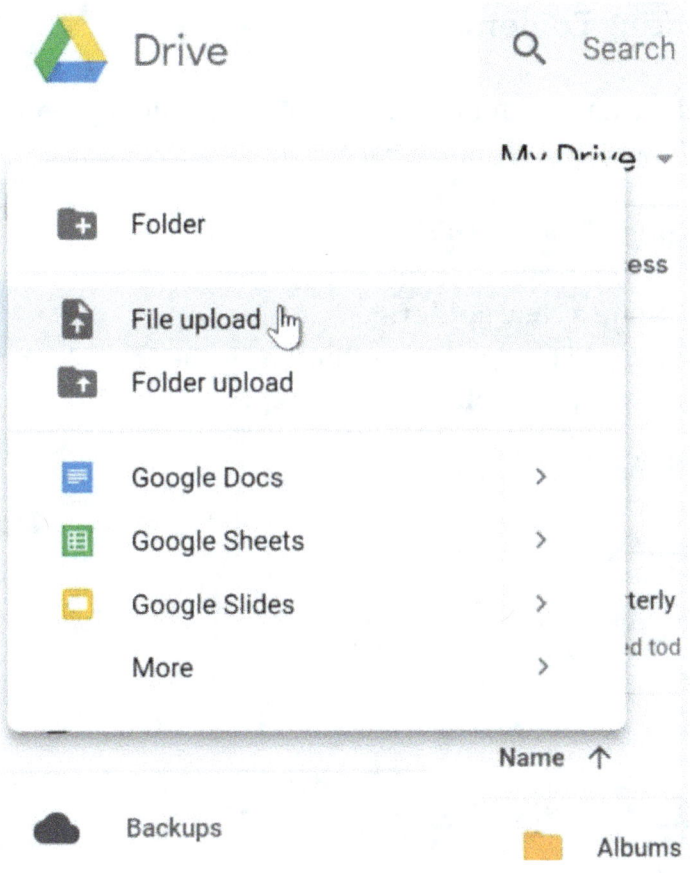

- o To upload entire folders: Select **Folder Upload** and navigate to the folder you wish to upload.

3. **Confirm Upload**:
   - o Once selected, the file(s) or folder(s) will begin uploading.
   - o A status bar in the bottom-right corner will show the progress and completion status.

2. Creating Folders

Folders are a powerful way to organize your files in Google Drive. Here's how to create and manage them:

Organizing Files into Folders

1. **Create a New Folder**:
   - Click the **+ New** button in the top-left corner and select **Folder**.

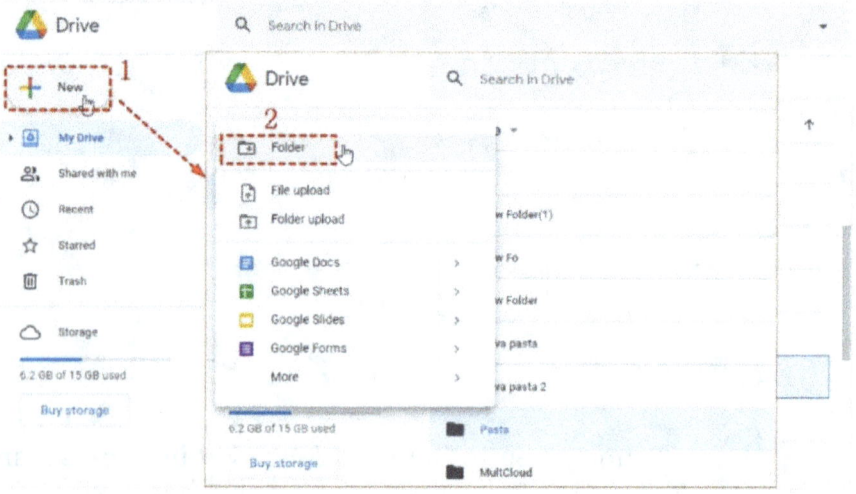

   - Enter a name for the folder and press **Create**.

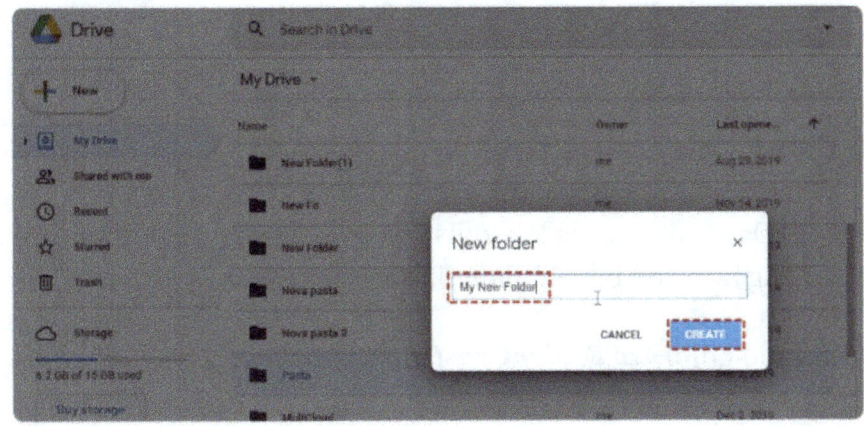

2. **Move Files into Folders**:
   - Drag and drop files from the file list into the folder.
   - Alternatively, right-click the file, select **Move to**, and choose the destination folder.
3. **Accessing Folders**:
   - Click the folder name in the navigation pane on the left or locate it in the file list.

Renaming, Moving, and Deleting Folders

1. **Rename Folders**:
   - Right-click the folder you want to rename and select **Rename**.
   - Enter the new name and press **Enter** or click **OK**.
2. **Move Folders**:
   - Right-click the folder and select **Move to**.
   - Choose the destination folder or create a new one.
3. **Delete Folders**:
   - Right-click the folder and select **Remove**.

- o Deleted folders will move to the **Trash**, where they can be restored or permanently deleted.

3. Using Colors and Labels

Google Drive offers visual tools like colors and labels to make managing files and folders more intuitive.

Assigning Colors to Folders for Easy Identification

1. **Change Folder Color**:
   - o Right-click the folder and select **Change Color** from the dropdown menu.
   - o Choose a color from the palette to apply it to the folder.

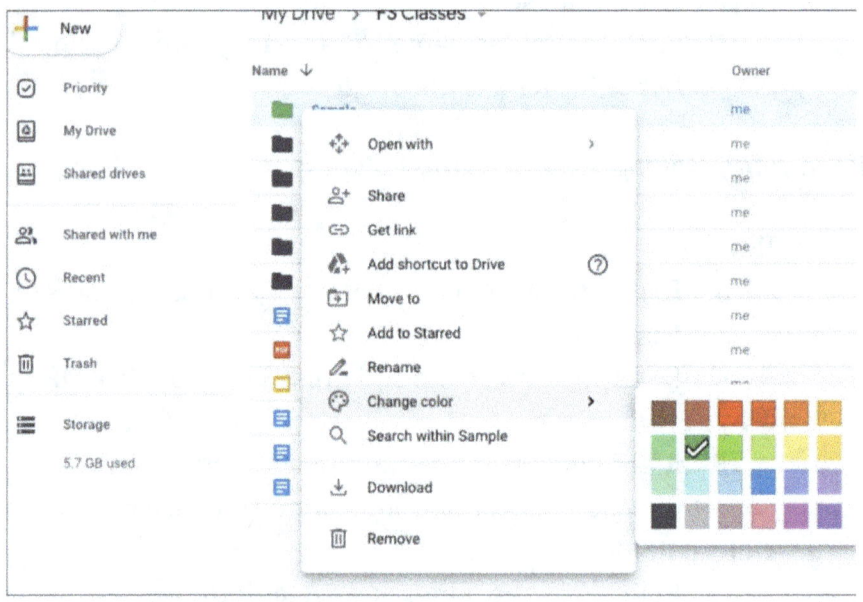

2. **Benefits of Using Colors**:

- Assign different colors for specific categories (e.g., red for work, blue for personal files).
- Quickly locate folders visually, even in a long list.

Using the "Starred" Feature for Important Files

1. **Mark Files as Starred**:
   - Right-click the file or folder you want to prioritize and select **Add to Starred**.
   - Alternatively, click the star icon next to the file name in the file list.

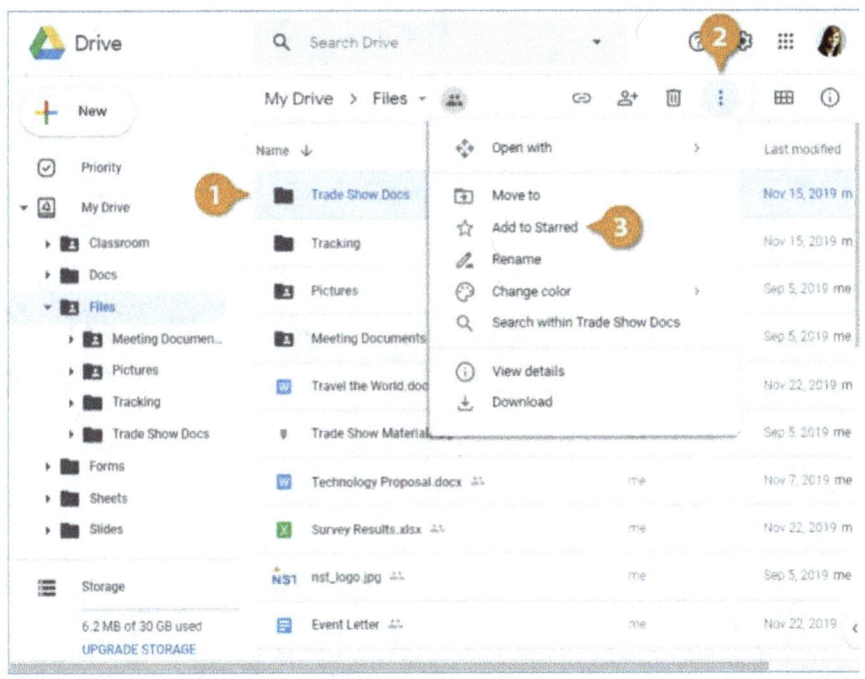

2. **Access Starred Files**:
   - Click **Starred** in the navigation pane on the left.

- o All files and folders marked as important will appear here.

3. **Remove Starred Status**:
   - o Right-click the file or folder in the Starred section and select **Remove from Starred**.

Chapter 3: Creating and Editing Files

1. Introduction to Google Workspace Apps

Google Drive integrates seamlessly with the suite of Google Workspace apps, making it easy to create, edit, and collaborate on files in real-time. Let's explore these apps:

Overview of Google Docs, Sheets, Slides, and Forms

1. **Google Docs**:
   - **Purpose**: Google Docs is an online word processor for creating and editing text documents.
   - **Key Features**:
     - Real-time collaboration with multiple users.
     - Auto-save feature to prevent loss of data.
     - Access to a variety of templates for reports, resumes, and more.
2. **Google Sheets**:
   - **Purpose**: Google Sheets is a spreadsheet tool for organizing data, performing calculations, and creating charts.
   - **Key Features**:
     - Built-in formulas and functions for calculations.
     - Data validation tools for input control.
     - Charts and graphs for visualizing data.
3. **Google Slides**:

- Purpose: Google Slides is used to create presentations, similar to Microsoft PowerPoint.
- Key Features:
  - Multiple templates for different presentation styles.
  - Transitions and animations for enhancing presentations.
  - Collaboration features that allow multiple users to edit slides simultaneously.

4. **Google Forms**:
   - Purpose: Google Forms is a tool for creating surveys, quizzes, and data collection forms.
   - Key Features:
     - Customizable templates for different types of forms.
     - Real-time response tracking with automatic data collection in Google Sheets.
     - Options to share forms via email or embedded links.

2. Creating New Files

Google Drive makes it easy to create files from scratch or by using pre-made templates. Here's how to do it:

Starting a Blank Document or Using Templates

1. **Creating a New Blank Document**:
   - Click the **+ New** button in the top-left corner of Google Drive.

- Select **Google Docs** for a word document, **Google Sheets** for a spreadsheet, **Google Slides** for a presentation, or **Google Forms** for a form.

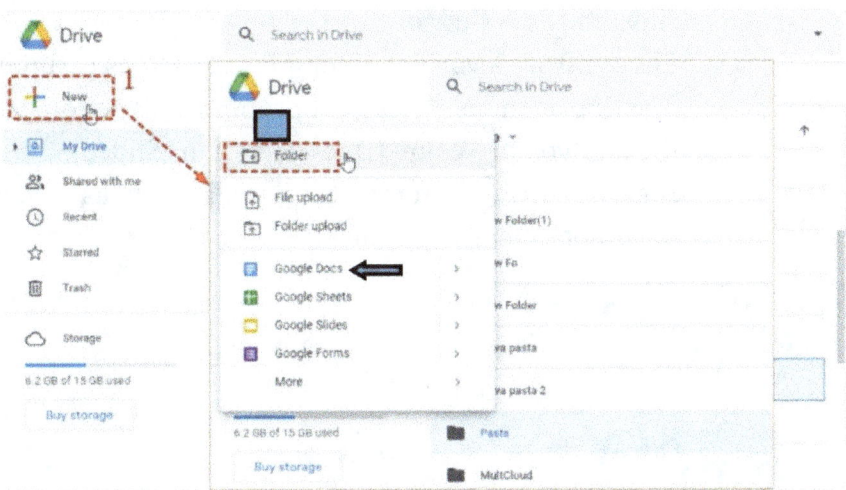

- A new file will open in a new tab, ready for you to start working on.

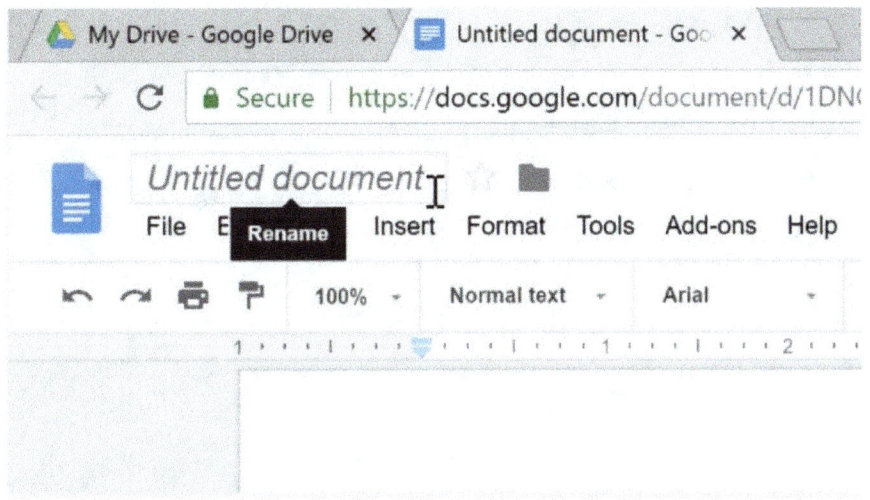

2. **Using Templates**:
   - ○ Instead of starting from scratch, you can use templates provided by Google.
   - ○ Click on the **Template Gallery** in the top-right corner (next to the **+ New** button).
   - ○ Choose from a variety of templates, such as resumes, meeting agendas, or project proposals, depending on the app you are using (Docs, Sheets, or Slides).
   - ○ After selecting a template, it will open as a new document where you can edit the content.

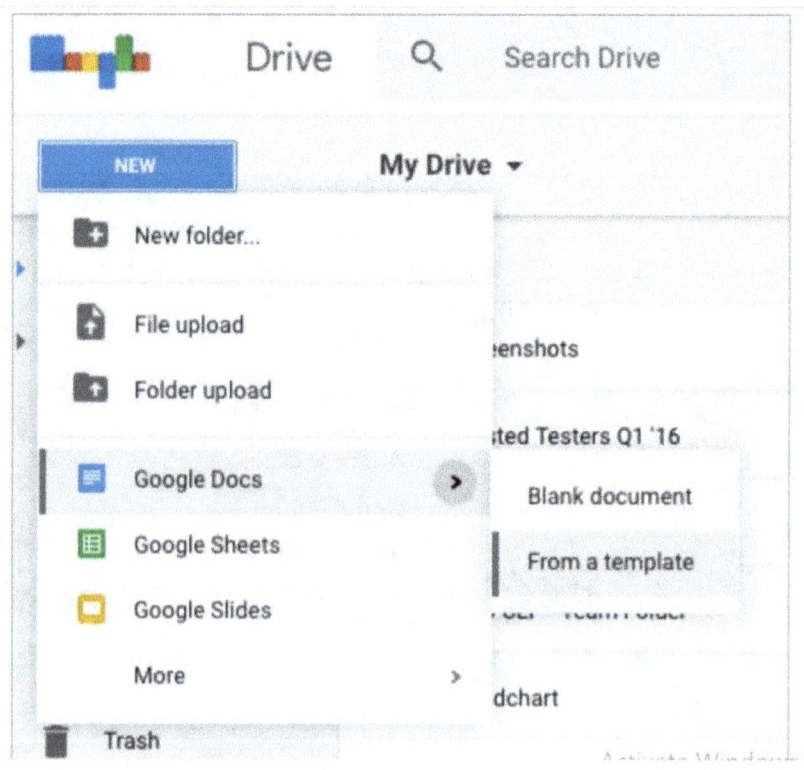

Saving Files in Different Formats (PDF, Word, etc.)

1. **Download Options**:
   - Once you have finished working on a file, you may want to save it in a different format for sharing or offline use.
   - To download a file, click **File** in the top-left menu and select **Download**.
   - For **Google Docs**:
     - You can choose from formats such as **Microsoft Word (.docx)**, **PDF Document (.pdf)**, **Plain Text (.txt)**, and more.
   - For **Google Sheets**:
     - Download as **Microsoft Excel (.xlsx)**, **PDF**, or **CSV** files, among others.
   - For **Google Slides**:
     - Download as **Microsoft PowerPoint (.pptx)**, **PDF**, or as a set of image files (JPG, PNG).
   - For **Google Forms**:
     - Download responses as **CSV** or export them directly to **Google Sheets** for analysis.
2. **Automatic Save**:
   - Google Drive automatically saves your files in Google's cloud storage. So, there's no need to manually save your work – it's always up-to-date.

3. Basic Editing Tips

Editing your files in Google Docs, Sheets, Slides, and Forms is easy with a variety of built-in tools and options. Here are some basic editing tips:

Adding Text, Images, and Tables

1. **Adding Text**:
    - Simply click anywhere within the document or spreadsheet and start typing.
    - Use the formatting toolbar at the top to adjust font styles, sizes, and colors.
2. **Adding Images**:
    - In **Google Docs** or **Google Slides**:
        - Click **Insert** in the top menu, then choose **Image**.
        - You can upload an image from your computer, search the web, or insert from Google Drive, Google Photos, or a URL.
    - In **Google Sheets**:
        - Images can be inserted directly into cells by selecting a cell and clicking **Insert > Image > Image in Cell** or **Image over Cells**.
3. **Adding Tables**:
    - In **Google Docs**:
        - Click **Insert** in the top menu, then select **Table** and choose the number of rows and columns.
    - In **Google Sheets**:
        - Tables are essentially the grid structure of the spreadsheet, and you can easily add rows and columns by right-clicking a row/column header and selecting **Insert row** or **Insert column**.

Formatting Options and Shortcuts

1. **Formatting Options**:
   - **Font Style**: Use the **Font** dropdown in the toolbar to select from a variety of font types.
   - **Font Size**: Adjust the font size using the **Font Size** dropdown next to the font style.
   - **Bold, Italic, and Underline**: Use the **B**, **I**, and **U** buttons in the toolbar or use keyboard shortcuts:
     - **Ctrl + B** (Windows) or **Cmd + B** (Mac) for bold.
     - **Ctrl + I** (Windows) or **Cmd + I** (Mac) for italics.
     - **Ctrl + U** (Windows) or **Cmd + U** (Mac) for underline.
2. **Using Shortcuts**:
   - **Undo and Redo**:
     - Press **Ctrl + Z** (Windows) or **Cmd + Z** (Mac) to undo the last action.
     - Press **Ctrl + Y** (Windows) or **Cmd + Y** (Mac) to redo.
   - **Text Alignment**: Click the alignment buttons in the toolbar to align your text to the left, center, or right.
   - **Bullets and Numbering**: Use the bullet or numbered list buttons to create organized lists.
3. **Applying Styles**:
   - In **Google Docs**, you can apply styles for headings, subheadings, and normal text.
   - In the toolbar, use the **Styles** dropdown to choose from **Heading 1**, **Heading 2**, etc., which helps create a consistent and structured document.

Chapter 4: File Sharing and Permissions

Google Drive makes it easy to collaborate with others by sharing files and folders. In this chapter, we'll explore how to share files, understand permission levels, and follow best practices for secure sharing.

1. Sharing Files and Folders

Sharing files and folders with others is a core feature of Google Drive. There are multiple ways to share, allowing you to choose the method that best suits your needs.

Sending Files via Links

1. **Sharing a Link to a File or Folder**:
   - Open Google Drive and locate the file or folder you want to share.
   - Right-click on the file or folder and select **Copy link** from the **Share** option.
   - A dialog box will appear, showing the link to the file. By default, the link will only be accessible to people who have been invited.
   - To change this, click on the **Anyone with the link** dropdown menu. From here, you can adjust who has access:
     - **Restricted**: Only people explicitly invited can view the file.

- **Anyone with the link**: Anyone who has the link can view or interact with the file, depending on permissions you set.
  - After setting the appropriate permissions, click **Copy link** to copy the link to your clipboard, which you can share through email, chat, or any other communication method.

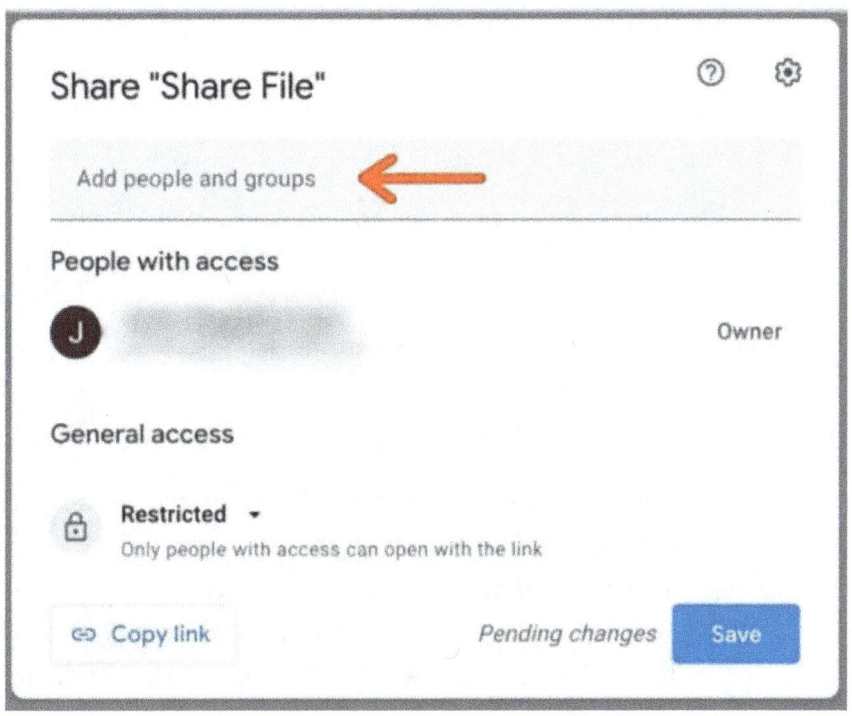

2. **Sharing Specific Files or Folders**:
   - If you're sharing a file that you want others to easily access without logging into Google Drive, simply copy the link and send it to them via email or text message.
   - You can also use this method to share folders, making it easier to share a collection of files.

Sharing through Email Invitations

1. **Inviting Specific People via Email:**
   o   Right-click on the file or folder and select **Share**.

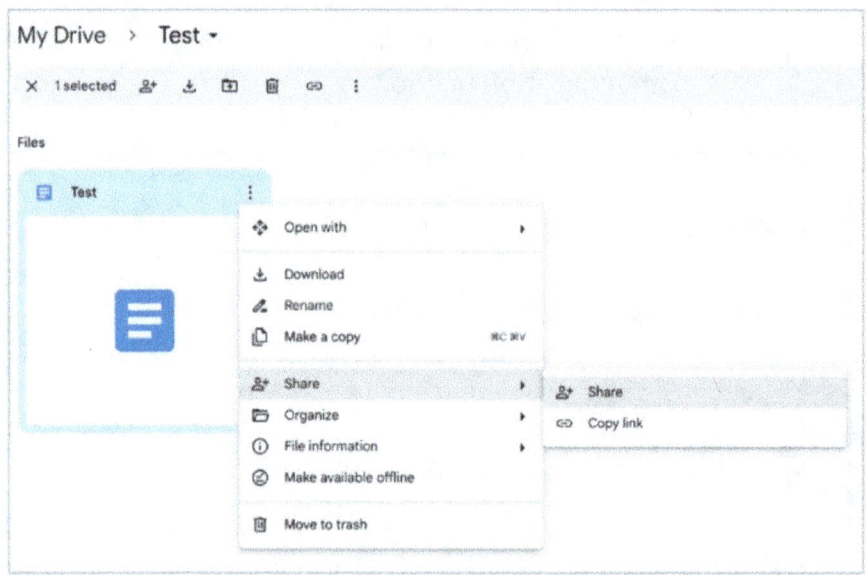

   o   In the sharing dialog, enter the email addresses of the people you want to share the file with.
   o   You can add multiple people at once.
   o   Before sending the invitation, you can choose the level of access they will have (more on that in the next section).
2. **Inviting External Users:**
   o   You can also invite external users (non-Google account users) by entering their email address. They will receive an invitation to view or edit the file.

- o If the recipient doesn't have a Google account, they may still be able to view or comment on the file depending on the permissions set.

3. **Personalizing the Invitation**:
   - o After entering the email addresses, you can write a personal message in the invitation box before sending the invite.
   - o This is useful if you want to explain why you are sharing the file and what you expect from the recipient.

2. Permission Levels

Google Drive allows you to assign different roles to people when sharing files or folders. This helps you control what others can do with your files, whether they are collaborators, viewers, or just recipients.

Viewer, Commenter, and Editor Roles

1. **Viewer**:
   - o People with **Viewer** access can only view the file or folder. They cannot make changes, add comments, or share the file with others.
   - o This is useful when you just want someone to read the document without the ability to alter it.

2. **Commenter**:
   - o A **Commenter** can view the document and add comments but cannot edit the actual content. This is useful for collaborative review processes where you

want feedback but don't want the person making changes to the file.

3. **Editor**:
   - An **Editor** has full access to modify the content of the file. Editors can add, delete, or change text, images, and other elements.
   - Editors can also share the file with others (unless restricted by higher-level permissions).

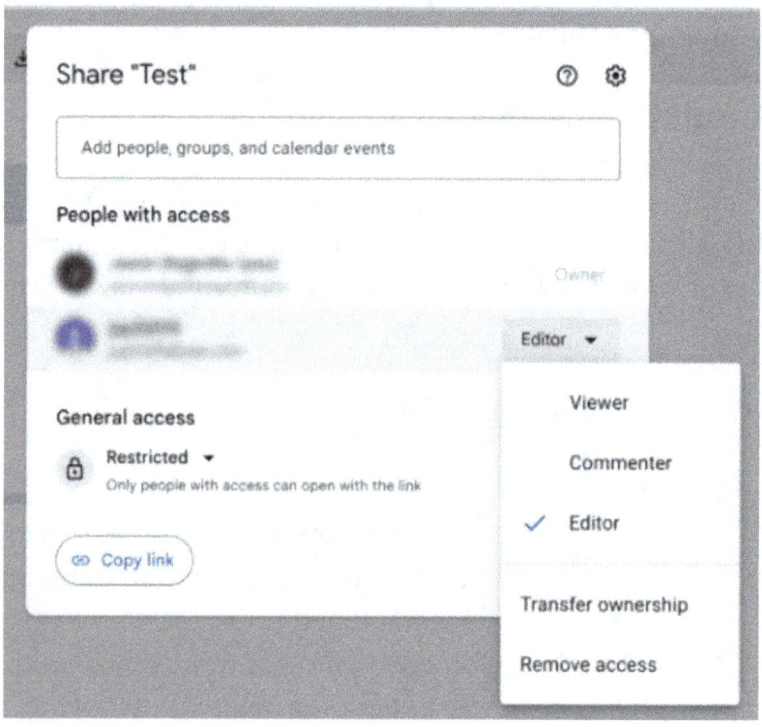

Managing Permissions for Multiple Users

1. **Assigning Permissions Individually**:
   - In the **Share** dialog, under **Share with people and groups**, you can assign individual permissions to

each person you invite by selecting their role from the dropdown list (Viewer, Commenter, or Editor).

2. **Changing Permissions for Existing Collaborators**:
   - To change someone's permissions after they have been invited, open the **Share** dialog, find the user's name or email, and click the **pencil icon** (Editor), **speech bubble icon** (Commenter), or **eye icon** (Viewer) next to their name.
   - From here, you can update their permission level.
3. **Removing Users**:
   - In the **Share** dialog, you can also remove people from the file by clicking the **trash can icon** next to their name. This will revoke their access to the file.

3. Best Practices for Sharing

While sharing files on Google Drive is easy and convenient, it's important to follow best practices to ensure that your files are secure and that you only share them with the right people.

Sharing Securely and Avoiding Unauthorized Access

1. **Limit Access to Trusted People**:
   - Always make sure you share files with trusted people and limit access to only those who need it. Be cautious when using the **Anyone with the link** option, as it allows anyone who has the link to view or interact with your file.
   - When possible, use **Restricted** settings to ensure that only specific individuals or groups can access the file.

2. **Use the "Viewer" Role for Sensitive Files**:
   - For files containing sensitive or confidential information, set the permission to **Viewer** for anyone you share them with. This ensures that others cannot edit or delete the content.
   - You can also apply this setting when sharing reports or presentations that you want others to read but not alter.
3. **Monitor Activity**:
   - Google Drive allows you to monitor the activity on shared files. You can view the **Activity dashboard** (found in the "View Details" section when right-clicking on a file) to see who has viewed or edited your file.
   - This helps you keep track of collaborators and maintain control over who is interacting with your documents.
4. **Set Expiration Dates for Access**:
   - If you only want someone to have temporary access to a file, you can set an **expiration date** for their permissions. To do this, open the **Share** dialog, click on the person's name, and choose **Set expiration**.
   - This is especially useful for contractors, temporary collaborators, or anyone who only needs short-term access.
5. **Disable Download, Print, or Copy Permissions**:
   - When sharing sensitive files, you may want to restrict recipients from downloading, printing, or copying the content. This option can be set for **Viewers** and **Commenters**.

o   To enable this, go to the **Share** dialog, click the gear icon in the top-right corner, and uncheck the box for **Viewers and Commenters can see the option to download, print, and copy**.

6. **Check Permissions Regularly**:
   o   Over time, you may forget who has access to your files. It's a good practice to periodically review your file's permissions and remove any users who no longer need access.
   o   You can do this by opening the **Share** dialog and reviewing the list of people with access. Remove anyone who should no longer have access.

Chapter 5: Collaboration Tools

Google Drive offers powerful collaboration features, making it easy to work with others on files and projects. In this chapter, we'll explore the tools that allow you to collaborate in real-time, manage file versions, and stay updated on changes through notifications.

1. Real-Time Collaboration

One of the key benefits of Google Drive is its ability to allow multiple people to work on the same file at the same time. This feature fosters teamwork, ensuring that everyone is on the same page and can contribute efficiently.

Working on Files Simultaneously with Others

1. **Opening and Sharing a File for Collaboration**:
    o   To begin collaborating in real-time, open the file you want to work on (e.g., a Google Docs document, Google Sheets spreadsheet, or Google Slides presentation).
    o   Share the file with your collaborators by clicking the **Share** button in the top-right corner and adding their email addresses or sharing a link.
2. **Seeing Other Users in Real-Time**:
    o   Once your collaborators have access to the file, you'll see their names or profile pictures in the top-right corner of the document (for Google Docs, Sheets, or Slides).

- o As your collaborators make changes, their cursor will be highlighted in different colors. This allows you to track what everyone is doing at any given moment.
- o Changes are automatically saved and updated in real-time, so there's no need to worry about manually saving your progress.

3. **Working Simultaneously on Google Docs, Sheets, and Slides**:
   - o **Google Docs**: Multiple users can edit the same document, add text, format paragraphs, and insert images.
   - o **Google Sheets**: Collaborators can enter data into cells, adjust formulas, and sort data. Google Sheets even allows users to comment on specific cells.
   - o **Google Slides**: When collaborating on a presentation, multiple users can edit the slides, add new ones, and update text, images, and layouts.

Commenting, Suggesting, and Resolving Changes

1. **Commenting**:
   - o Google Drive allows you to comment on specific sections of a document. This feature is especially helpful when reviewing documents and providing feedback.
   - o To comment in Google Docs, Sheets, or Slides, highlight the text or element you want to comment on, right-click, and select **Comment**.

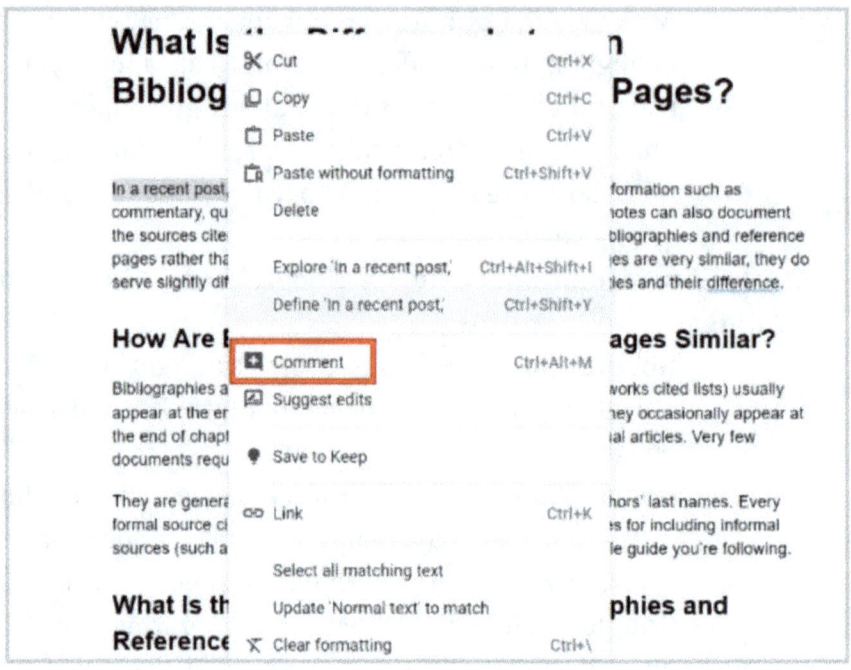

o Type your comment and click **Comment** to save it.

- o Collaborators can reply to comments, making it easy to discuss changes directly within the document.

2. **Suggesting Edits**:
   - o In Google Docs, you can switch to **Suggesting Mode** by clicking on the pencil icon in the top-right corner and selecting **Suggesting**.
   - o In this mode, any changes you make will be displayed as suggestions (instead of being applied directly). Other collaborators can review the suggestions and either accept or reject them.
   - o This helps maintain a record of proposed changes and ensures that everyone agrees on edits before they're made permanent.

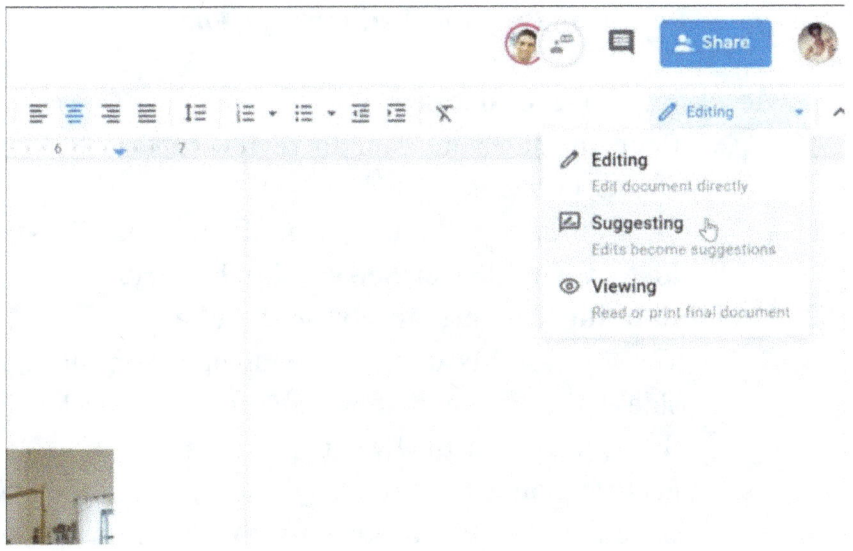

3. **Resolving Changes**:

- o Once a suggestion has been accepted or rejected, the comment thread will be closed, and the change will be reflected in the document.
- o To resolve a comment, click the **Checkmark** icon next to it. This removes the comment from the sidebar and marks it as resolved.

2. Version History

Google Drive automatically saves the changes made to your files and keeps a detailed record of all the edits made by collaborators. This feature is invaluable when you want to revert to an earlier version of a file or track how a document has evolved over time.

Viewing and Restoring Previous Versions of a File

1. **Accessing Version History**:
   - o Open the file you want to review in Google Docs, Sheets, or Slides.
   - o Click on **File** in the top menu, then select **Version history**, and click on **See version history**.
2. **Understanding the Version History Sidebar**:
   - o The **Version history** panel will appear on the right side of the screen. It shows all the saved versions of the document, listed by date and time.
   - o Each version will also display who made the changes, so you can see who contributed to the file at different stages.
3. **Restoring a Previous Version**:
   - o To restore a previous version, simply click on the version you want to revert to in the sidebar.

- You can review the changes made in that version. If you decide to revert, click the **Restore this version** button.
- Google Drive will replace the current version with the selected one, but you can always view the current version again by returning to the version history.

4. **Naming Versions**:
- If you want to mark a significant version (such as a draft, final, or review stage), you can name it for easy reference.
- In the version history panel, click on the three vertical dots next to a version and select **Name this version**. Enter a name that reflects the version's purpose or milestone.

5. **Previewing Changes Between Versions**:
- You can also compare the differences between two versions of a file by selecting two versions in the version history sidebar. Google Drive will highlight the changes, showing what was added or removed between those versions.

3. Using Notifications

Google Drive's notification system helps you stay updated when someone makes changes to your shared files. This feature is useful for collaboration, as it keeps everyone informed of edits, comments, and suggestions.

Enabling Notifications for File Updates

1. **Setting Up Email Notifications**:
   - By default, Google Drive will send you email notifications when someone comments on your files or when someone shares a file with you.
   - To customize your notifications, open the file and click on the **Comments** button in the top-right corner (for Docs, Sheets, and Slides). Then, click on the **bell icon** to toggle notification settings.
   - You can select to receive notifications for:
     - **All comments**: Receive notifications for all comments on the document.
     - **Only comments directed at you**: Get notified only when you are mentioned in a comment.
     - **None**: Disable all comment-related notifications.

2. **Setting Notifications for Specific Changes**:
   - Google Drive also notifies you when someone shares a file with you or makes significant edits to a file you own or are collaborating on.
   - If you want more granular control over your notifications, click on the **Settings** icon (gear) in Google Drive and select **Settings**.

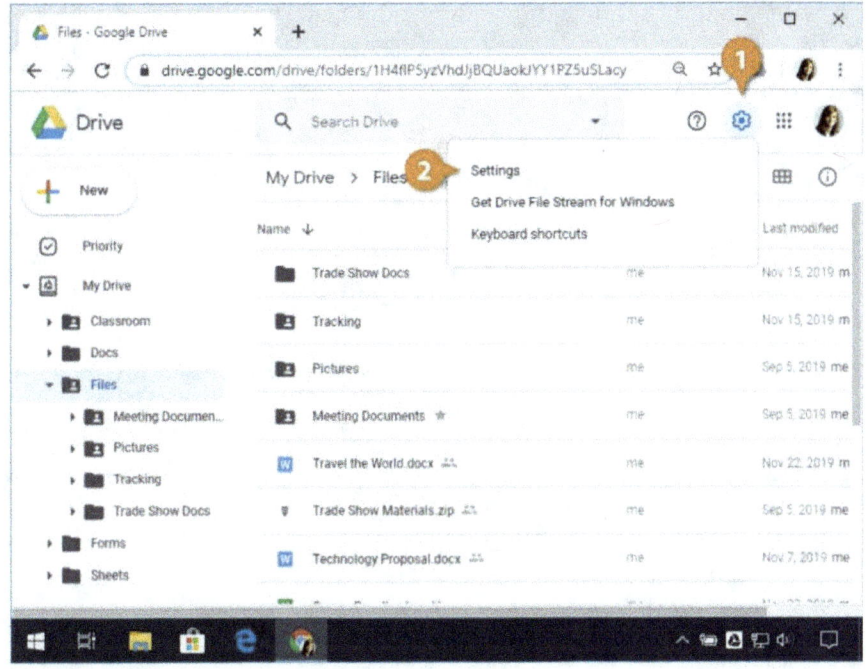

o   Go to **Notifications** tab. Here, you can select the types of updates you want to be notified about, such as new files shared with you or changes made to your files.

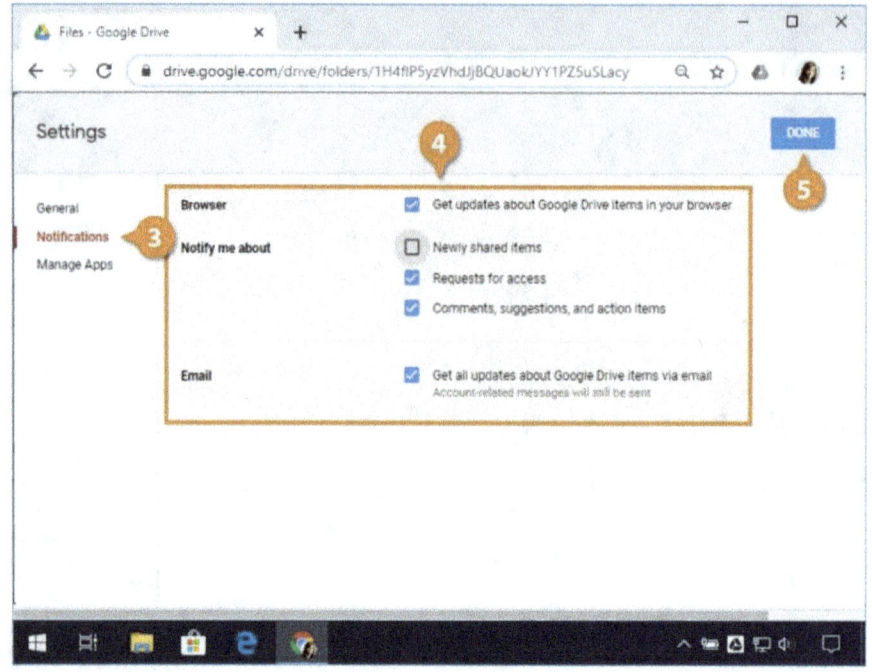

3. **Activity Dashboard**:
   - The **Activity dashboard** allows you to see who has viewed your file and when. To access it, open a file and click on **Tools** in the menu, then select **Activity dashboard**.
   - This feature helps you monitor who is actively engaging with your document, which is particularly useful when you need to follow up with collaborators or stakeholders.

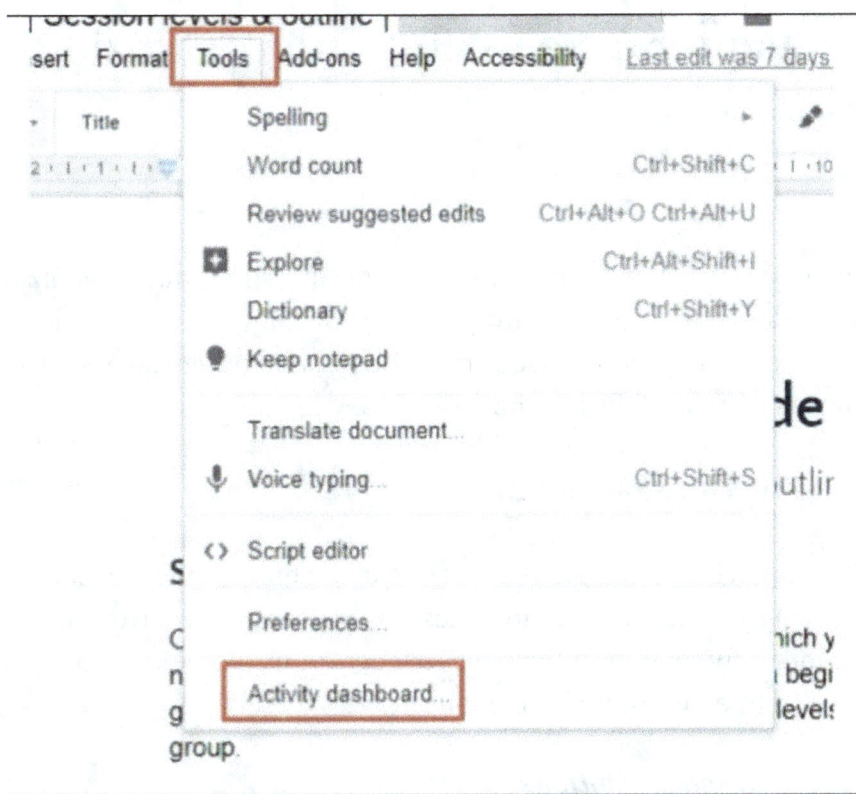

4. **Using Google Drive's Mobile App for Notifications**:
    - If you are using the Google Drive mobile app, notifications will appear as push notifications on your phone or tablet. You can adjust your notification preferences in the **Settings** section of the app by selecting **Notifications** and choosing whether you want to receive alerts for all activity or only specific updates.

Chapter 6: Searching and Organizing Files

Google Drive offers powerful tools for searching and organizing your files. This chapter will guide you through how to efficiently find and manage your documents, images, and other files, ensuring that everything stays organized and easy to access.

1. Using the Search Bar

The search bar in Google Drive is one of the most powerful features, allowing you to quickly find files based on various criteria. Let's explore how to use it effectively to locate your files, even when you have a large number of documents.

Advanced Search Options

1. **Accessing the Search Bar**:
   - The search bar is located at the top of the Google Drive interface. Click into the bar to begin typing your search terms.
2. **Performing a Basic Search**:
   - For a basic search, simply type a keyword related to the file you're looking for, such as a document name, phrase, or file type.
   - As you type, Google Drive will automatically suggest relevant files based on your search terms.
3. **Using Advanced Search**:

o To refine your search, click the **downward arrow** (also called the search options button) on the right side of the search bar.

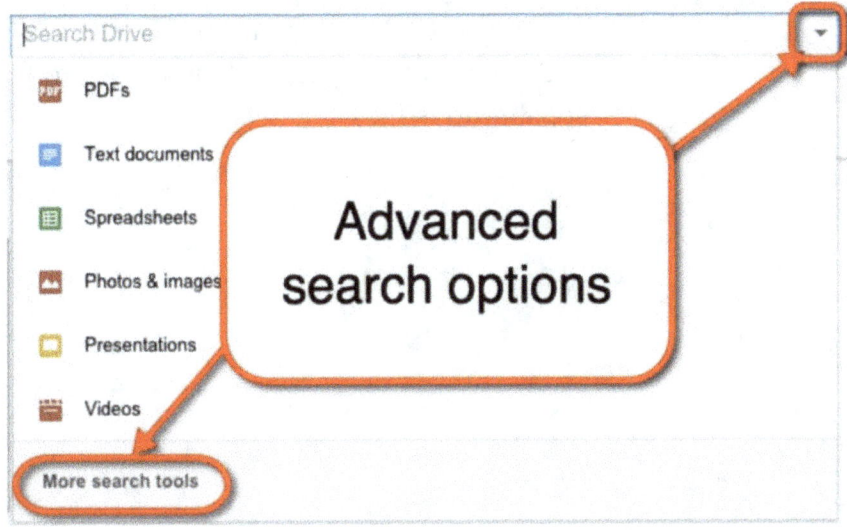

o This opens the advanced search menu, which allows you to filter results based on the following criteria:

- **Type**: Search for specific types of files, such as documents, spreadsheets, presentations, PDFs, images, etc.
- **Owner**: Find files owned by a specific person or organization. You can search by your own files or files shared with you.
- **Location**: Search within specific folders or locations in your Drive, such as "My Drive" or shared drives.
- **Date Modified**: Filter results by files modified within a specific date range. You can choose

from options like "Last 24 hours," "Last 7 days," or a custom date range.

- **Has the Words**: Search for files that contain specific keywords within the content.
- **Shared with Me**: Search for files that have been shared with you, making it easy to find collaborative files.

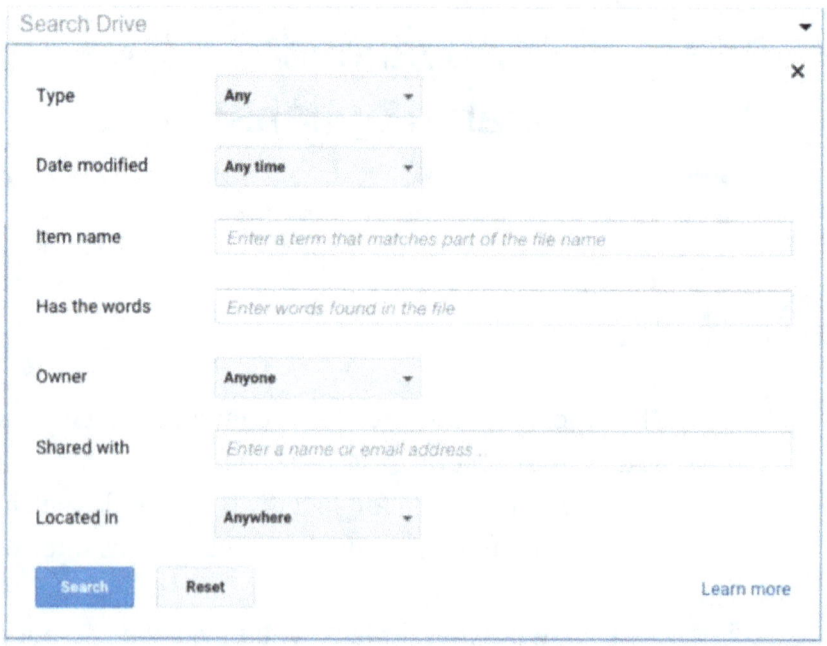

Click any of the dropdowns to select an item

4. **Using Search Operators**:
   - You can use specific search operators in the search bar to further refine your results. For example:
     - **owner:** to search for files owned by a specific person.

- **type:** to search for files of a specific type, e.g., type:spreadsheet or type:document.
- **before:** and **after:** to search for files created or modified before or after a certain date.

Filtering Files by Type, Owner, or Date

1. **Type**: To search for files of a specific type, click the **Search options** button and select from the dropdown list, such as "Documents," "Spreadsheets," "PDFs," etc. This will narrow your search results to files of that type.
2. **Owner**: If you are looking for files that were created or owned by a particular person, you can type the person's email address into the **Owner** field in the advanced search. This is helpful for finding shared documents or files from coworkers or collaborators.
3. **Date**: Use the **Date Modified** filter to focus on files changed within a particular period. This is useful when you need to find recent updates or older files that haven't been touched in a while.

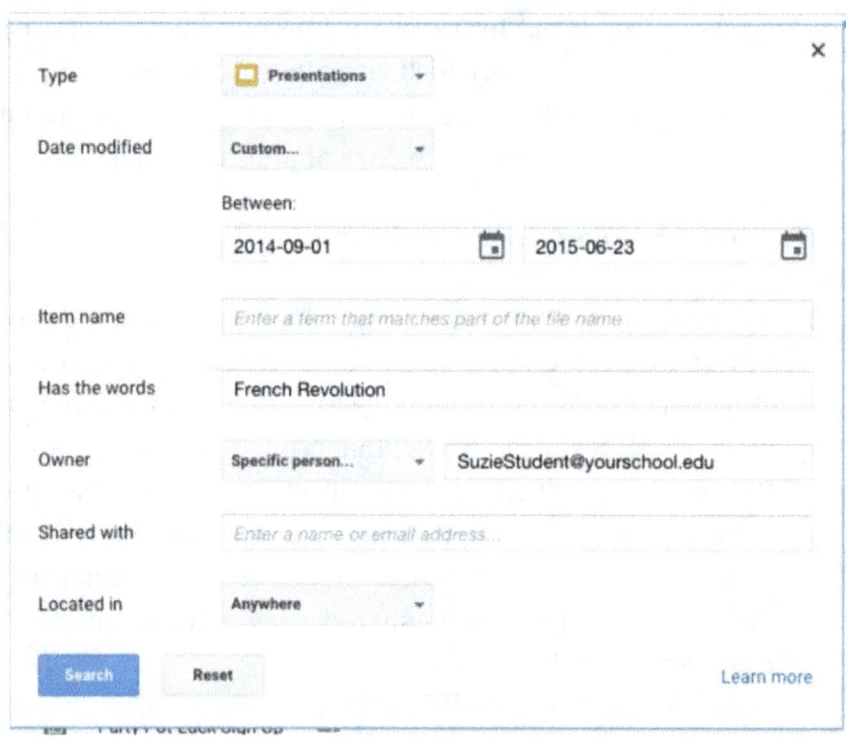

Type   Presentations

Date modified   Custom...

Between:

2014-09-01   2015-06-23

Item name   *Enter a term that matches part of the file name*

Has the words   French Revolution

Owner   Specific person...   SuzieStudent@yourschool.edu

Shared with   *Enter a name or email address...*

Located in   Anywhere

Search   Reset   Learn more

Example of search terms you can use

2. Organizing Files

To keep your Google Drive clutter-free and easy to navigate, it's important to organize your files effectively. Google Drive offers a variety of organizational tools that can help you maintain order in your documents.

Grouping Files into Folders

1. **Creating Folders**:

- To create a new folder, click the **New** button on the left side of your Google Drive interface and select **Folder**.

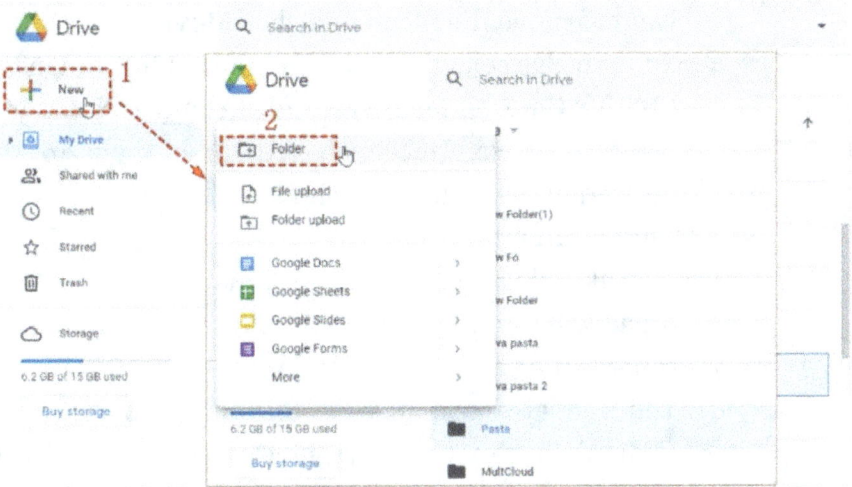

- Name your folder and click **Create**. This will create a new folder in your main Drive view, where you can store related files.

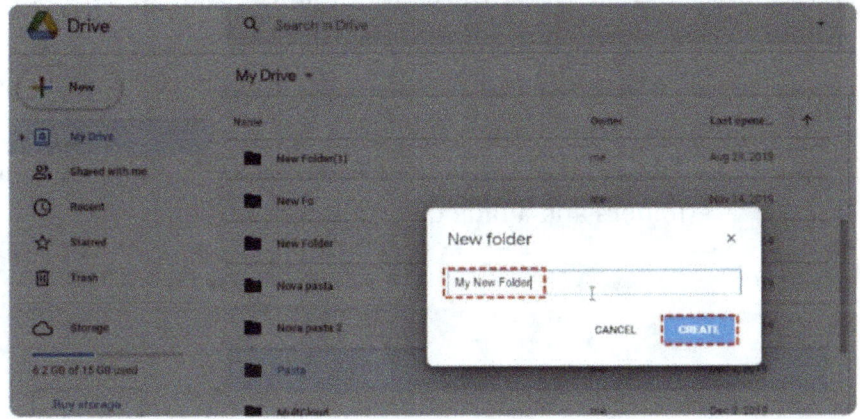

2. **Moving Files into Folders**:
   - To move files into a folder, simply drag and drop them into the folder. Alternatively, right-click on the file and select **Move to**. Then, choose the folder you want to move the file to and click **Move**.
   - You can also select multiple files by holding down the **Ctrl** (or **Cmd** on Mac) key and clicking each file you want to move. Once selected, drag them to the desired folder or use the **Move to** option.
3. **Organizing Folders**:
   - Just like files, folders can be renamed, moved, and organized as needed. Right-click on a folder to rename it or change its location.
   - You can also use **nested folders** (folders within folders) to create a more hierarchical organization system.

Using Tags or Descriptions

1. **Color-Coding Folders**:
   - A great way to visually organize your folders is by using color-coding. Right-click on a folder and select **Change color**. Choose a color to help categorize and visually distinguish folders from one another.
   - For example, use a green color for work-related folders and a blue color for personal ones.

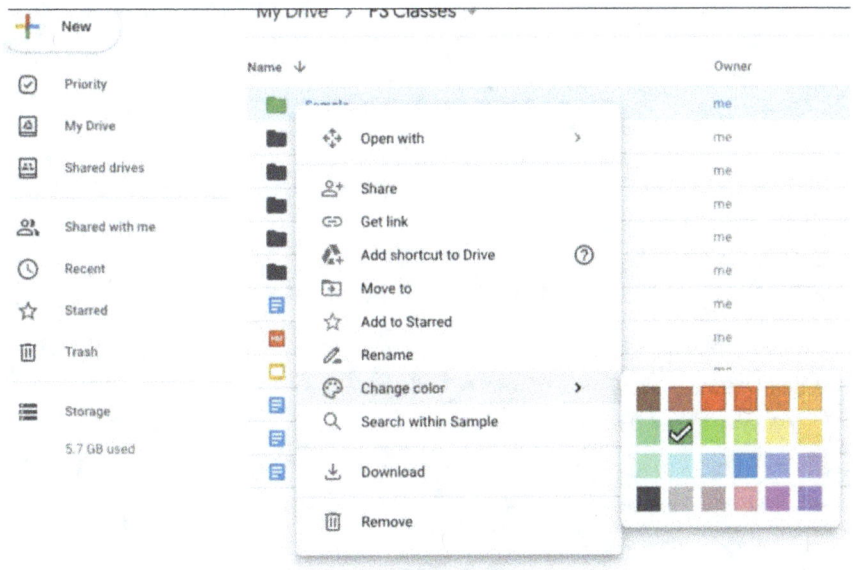

2. **Adding Descriptions to Files and Folders**:
    ○   While Google Drive does not have a built-in tagging feature, you can add descriptions to your files to make them easier to identify.
    ○   To add a description to a file or folder, right-click the item and select **View details**.

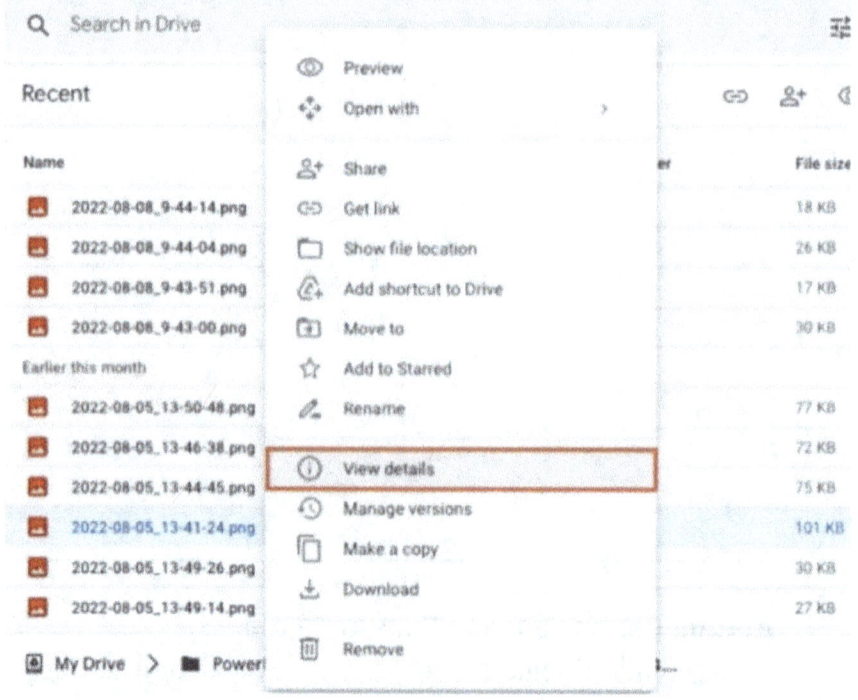

- In the details pane, you can type in a description under the **Description** section. This text will appear when you hover over the file, providing additional context for quick identification.

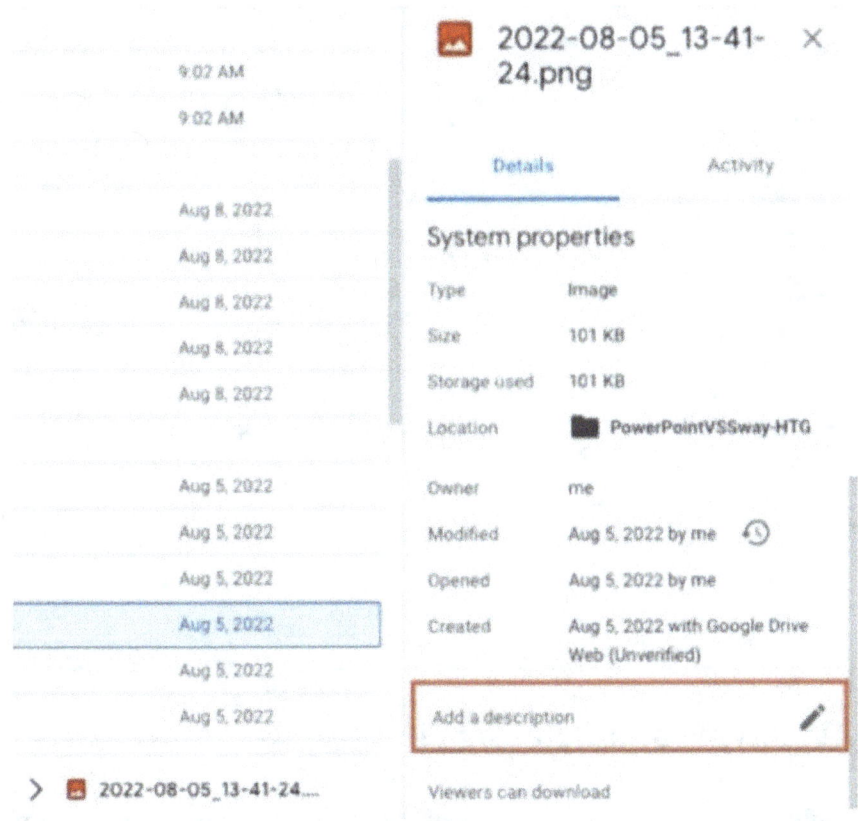

3. **Using the "Starred" Feature**:

    o If you have files that you need quick access to, use the
       Starred feature. Right-click on the file or folder and
       select **Add to Starred**. This will add it to the Starred
       section in the left-hand menu, making it easy to
       access frequently used files.

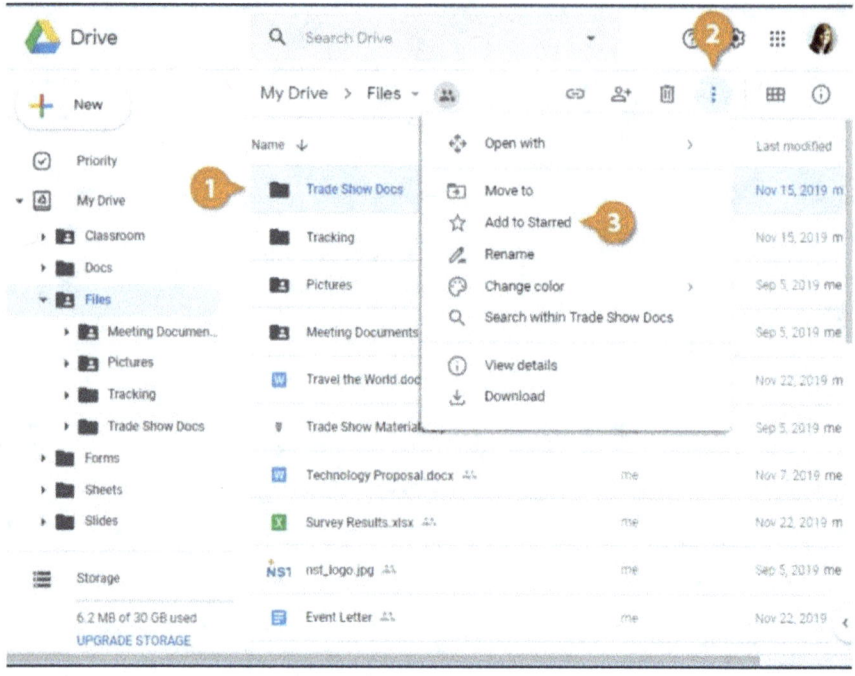

3. Archiving and Deleting Files

Google Drive provides an easy way to manage and remove unwanted files. It's important to know how to archive and delete files to keep your storage organized and make room for new ones.

Moving Files to Trash

1. **Deleting Files**:
    o To delete a file, right-click on it and select **Remove**. This will move the file to your **Trash** folder, which is essentially a holding area for deleted files.
    o If you want to delete multiple files at once, hold down the **Ctrl** (or **Cmd** on Mac) key and select each file. Then, right-click and choose **Remove**.

2. **Emptying the Trash**:
   - ○ Files in the Trash will remain there until you manually empty it. To do so, click on **Trash** in the left sidebar, then click **Empty trash** at the top of the page.
   - ○ Be aware that files in Trash will be automatically deleted after 30 days, but you can manually restore them if needed before that time.

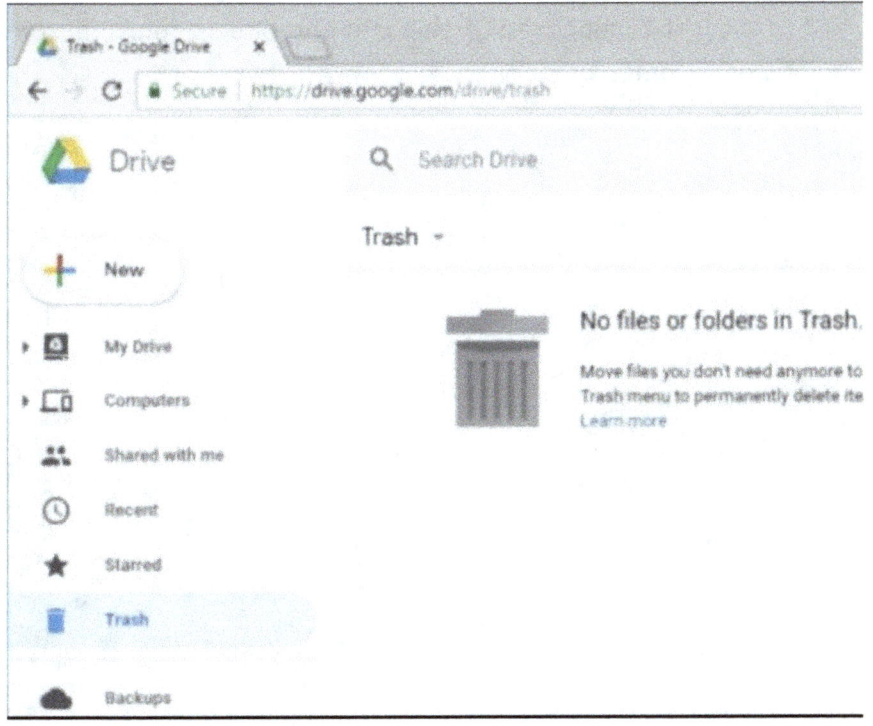

Recovering Deleted Files

1. **Restoring Files from Trash**:
   - ○ If you accidentally deleted a file, don't worry! You can recover it from Trash. Open the **Trash** folder, right-

click on the file you want to restore, and select **Restore**.

- The file will be restored to its original location in your Google Drive.

2. **Restoring Files Using Version History**:
   - If you need to recover an earlier version of a file that has been edited or deleted, use the **Version history** feature. This allows you to restore previous versions of a file even if the current one is missing some content.

Chapter 7: Syncing and Offline Access

Google Drive's syncing and offline access features allow you to work on your files seamlessly across different devices, both with and without an internet connection. This chapter will guide you through setting up syncing, enabling offline mode, and troubleshooting common issues that may arise while syncing your files.

1. Setting Up Syncing

Syncing ensures that your files are consistently updated across all your devices, so you can always access the latest version. This section will help you configure Google Drive's desktop app and customize which folders to sync.

Configuring the Desktop App

1. **Installing Google Drive for Desktop**:
    - If you haven't installed the desktop app yet, go to the Google Drive Download Page, and download the installer for your operating system (Windows or macOS).
    - Open the installer once it's downloaded and follow the prompts to complete the installation. Once installed, the app will automatically launch and prompt you to sign in with your Google account.
2. **Logging In and Setting Up the App**:
    - After installation, sign in to the app using your Google credentials. This will link the app to your Google

Drive account and allow the app to sync files between your computer and the cloud.

- o Choose your syncing preferences during the initial setup:
  - **Sync My Drive to this computer**: This option will sync all files and folders in your Google Drive to your computer.
  - **Sync only these folders**: If you have limited storage on your computer, you can select specific folders to sync instead of syncing everything.

3. **Accessing Your Files Locally**:
   - o Once syncing is complete, you can access your Google Drive files directly from your computer. These files are stored in a folder named "Google Drive," which is automatically created on your computer.
   - o You can open and work on these files just like you would with any other file on your computer.

Syncing Specific Folders Only

1. **Selective Sync**:
   - o If you only want to sync certain folders to your computer to save space, open the Google Drive settings by clicking the **Google Drive icon** in your system tray (Windows) or menu bar (macOS).
   - o Click **Preferences** in the menu, then navigate to the **Google Drive** tab. Under **My Drive syncing options**, you will see a list of your folders.
   - o Choose **Sync only these folders** and check the boxes next to the folders you want to sync. Any folders

unchecked will remain in the cloud and won't be stored locally on your device.

2. **Accessing Synced Folders**:
   - The folders you select to sync will appear in your Google Drive folder on your computer. These folders will automatically update as changes are made either on your computer or in the cloud.

2. Accessing Files Offline

With Google Drive's offline access feature, you can work on your files even when you don't have an internet connection. This section will guide you through enabling offline mode and editing your files offline.

Enabling Offline Mode

1. **Using Google Drive for Desktop for Offline Access**:
   - Once the desktop app is set up and syncing, files stored in your Google Drive folder will automatically be available offline. These files are synced with your cloud storage and can be edited without an internet connection.
   - For files to remain accessible offline, ensure they are selected for syncing as mentioned earlier. Any changes made offline will be synced to Google Drive the next time you are online.

2. **Using Google Drive on Mobile Devices**:
   - For mobile users, Google Drive offers offline access through the mobile app. Open the Google Drive app on your Android or iOS device.

- Find the file you want to access offline, then tap the **three-dot menu** next to it. Select **Available offline**. This will download the file to your device so that you can view and edit it without an internet connection.
- For offline access to folders, select the folder and mark it as available offline.

Editing Files Without an Internet Connection

1. **Working with Google Docs, Sheets, and Slides Offline**:
   - Once a file is downloaded for offline use, you can edit it just like you would online. Whether it's a document, spreadsheet, or presentation, any changes made will be saved locally until your device is connected to the internet again.
   - When you reconnect to the internet, Google Drive will automatically sync the changes made offline to the cloud.
2. **Using Google Drive for Desktop to Edit Offline**:
   - You can edit your synced Google Drive files directly from your desktop. Files that have been synced will open in the appropriate Google Workspace app (Docs, Sheets, Slides, etc.), and edits will be saved to the local version.
   - Once your device reconnects to the internet, these local changes will be synced back to your cloud storage, ensuring that your online and offline versions match.
3. **Managing Offline Files**:
   - To manage your offline files, open the Google Drive app on your mobile device or desktop. On mobile, you

can see which files are available offline in the "Offline" section. On the desktop app, the synced files are marked with a green check icon, indicating they are available offline.

3. Troubleshooting Sync Issues

Syncing problems can sometimes occur, but fortunately, most issues have straightforward solutions. This section will help you resolve common syncing problems.

Common Errors and Solutions

1. **Syncing is Stuck or Not Completing**:
   - **Solution**: Restart the Google Drive for Desktop app. If that doesn't work, sign out and sign back in. You can also try restarting your computer to reset the syncing process.
   - If the issue persists, check your internet connection to ensure that Google Drive has access to sync your files.
2. **Files Not Syncing or Showing Up**:
   - **Solution**: If you notice that certain files are not syncing, make sure they are selected for syncing in the app's preferences. Additionally, ensure there is enough storage space on both your local device and Google Drive to accommodate the files.
   - Sometimes, files with large sizes may take longer to sync. Ensure that your internet connection is stable and strong.
3. **Offline Files Not Syncing When Reconnecting**:

- o **Solution**: If files edited offline are not syncing back to the cloud after reconnecting to the internet, manually force a sync by right-clicking the Google Drive icon in the system tray or menu bar and selecting **Sync Now**. Also, check if your internet connection is stable.
- o If using the mobile app, ensure that the device is properly connected to Wi-Fi or cellular data.

4. **Error Messages Related to Storage Limits**:
   - o **Solution**: If you're receiving an error indicating you've reached your storage limit, check your Google Drive's storage usage. You may need to free up space by deleting old or unnecessary files, or you can upgrade to a higher storage plan if needed.

Chapter 8: Integrating with Google Services

Google Drive works seamlessly with other Google services, offering a wide range of features to enhance your productivity and streamline your workflow. This chapter will guide you through integrating Google Drive with Gmail, Google Photos, Google Calendar, and Google Keep, helping you make the most of your Google ecosystem.

1. Using Google Drive with Gmail

Gmail and Google Drive are deeply integrated, allowing you to attach Drive files to emails and store email attachments directly in Drive. This integration makes it easy to manage your files and emails in one place.

Attaching Drive Files to Emails

1. **Composing a New Email**:
   - Open Gmail in your browser or mobile app.
   - Click the **Compose** button to create a new email.
2. **Attaching Files from Google Drive**:
   - In the new email window, click the **Google Drive icon** at the bottom (it looks like a triangle).

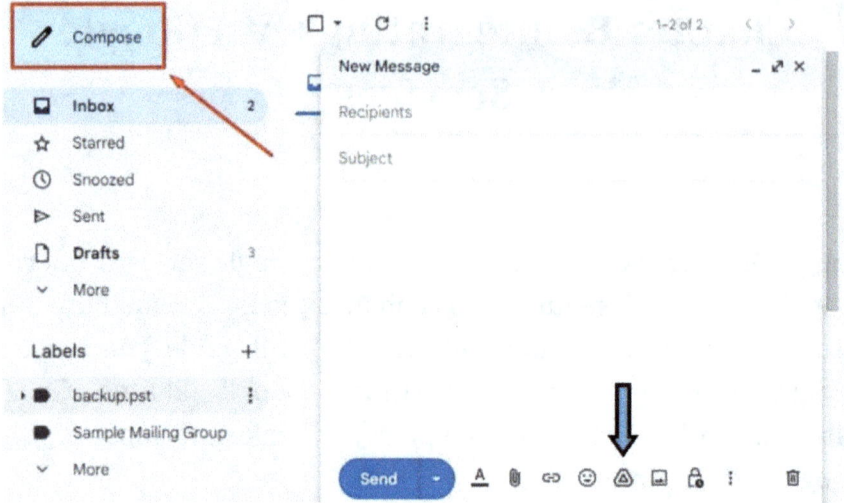

- o This will open a window showing all your Google Drive files.
- o Browse and select the file(s) you want to attach.
- o Click the **Insert** button to add the file as a Drive link. The recipient will be able to click on the link and access the file from Google Drive.

3. **Choosing Sharing Options**:
   - o When attaching a file from Drive, Gmail will prompt you to set the file's sharing permissions. You can select from the following options:
     - ▪ **Restricted**: Only specific people can view the file.
     - ▪ **Anyone with the link**: Anyone who has the link can view or edit the file, depending on your selection.
   - o Adjust the permissions as needed before sending the email.

4. **Sending the Email**:

- After attaching the file, compose your message and hit **Send**. The recipient will receive an email with a link to the file, and you can always manage the permissions afterward from Google Drive.

Saving Email Attachments Directly to Drive

1. **Opening the Email**:
   - When you receive an email with an attachment, open the email in Gmail.
2. **Saving Attachments to Google Drive**:
   - Hover over the email attachment, and you will see a **Google Drive icon** appear on the right side of the attachment preview.
   - Click on the **Google Drive icon**, and the attachment will be saved directly to your Google Drive.
3. **Organizing the Saved Attachment**:
   - You can choose a specific folder in Google Drive to save the attachment or let it default to the main Drive folder.
   - Once saved, the file will be available in your Drive, where you can access and organize it as needed.

2. Google Photos Integration

Google Photos allows you to back up, store, and organize your photos and videos in the cloud. You can also access and manage your media files directly from Google Drive.

Backing Up Photos to Drive

1. **Setting Up Google Photos Backup**:
   - Open the **Google Photos** app on your phone or go to the [Google Photos website](https://photos.google.com/) at https://photos.google.com/ in a web browser.
   - Ensure that **Backup & Sync** is turned on. This will automatically upload all your photos and videos to Google Photos, and you can access them through Google Drive.
2. **Organizing Your Photos**:
   - As your photos are uploaded, they will be organized in **Albums** based on date, location, or people.
   - If you prefer, you can manually create albums and arrange your photos in a way that makes sense to you.
3. **Accessing Photos from Google Drive**:
   - Google Photos and Google Drive are linked, and photos and videos uploaded to Google Photos can be viewed and organized within Google Drive.
   - Open **Google Drive** in a browser or the app, and you will find a folder called **Google Photos**. This folder contains your uploaded photos and videos, allowing you to manage and share them just like any other file.
4. **Managing Photos within Drive**:
   - You can move photos from Google Photos to other folders within Google Drive, but they will remain synced with the Google Photos library for easy access.
   - Photos stored in Google Drive can be shared, edited, and organized with folders like any other files.

3. Integrating with Calendar and Keep

Google Calendar and Google Keep are powerful tools for managing events and notes. By integrating these services with Google Drive, you can streamline your scheduling and note-taking processes.

Linking Drive Files to Calendar Events

1. **Creating a New Event in Google Calendar**:
   - Open **Google Calendar** and create a new event by clicking the **+ Create** button.

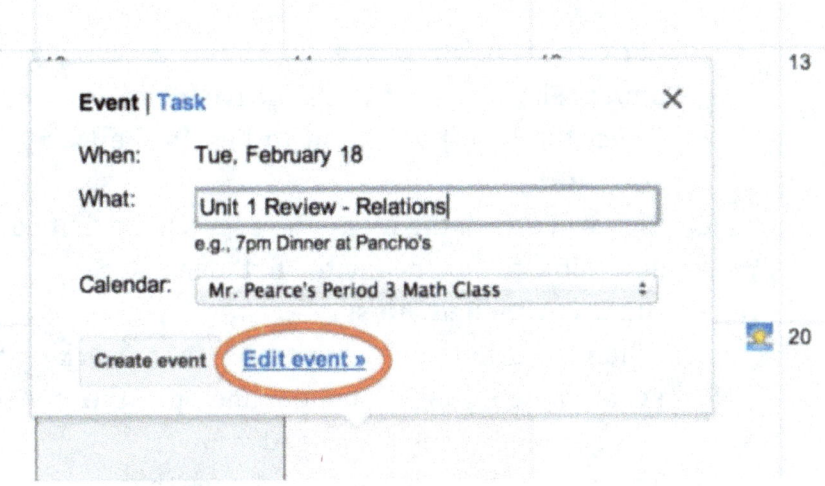

2. **Adding Files from Google Drive**:
   - In the event details window, scroll to the **Add attachment** section.

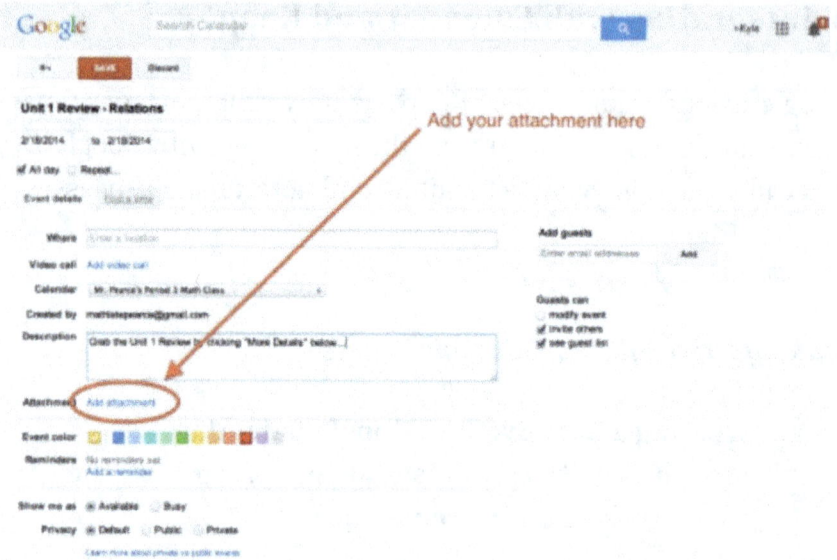

- o Click the **Google Drive icon**, and a window will appear showing your Google Drive files.
- o Select the file(s) you want to link to the event and click **Add**.
- o This will attach the file to the event, making it easily accessible to anyone invited to the event.
3. **Accessing the Attached Files**:
   - o When the event occurs, participants can click on the event in their Google Calendar and open the attached file(s) directly from the calendar invite.
   - o The file is linked, and you can change the permissions in Google Drive if you need to share the file with others.

Using Keep for Notes and File References

1. **Creating Notes in Google Keep**:

- Open the **Google Keep** app or go to Google Keep at https://keep.google.com/ in a browser.
- Click on **Take a note** to start creating a new note.

2. **Adding Drive Files to Keep Notes**:
   - While creating a note, click the **Google Drive icon** to add a file from your Drive.
   - This can be particularly useful for keeping track of documents you're working on, reminders for specific files, or links to files you reference often.

3. **Using Keep for File References**:
   - You can create a note with a link to a specific Google Drive file, allowing you to easily access or share files with others.
   - Keep allows you to organize notes with labels and colors, making it easy to refer to specific files or notes related to different projects.

4. **Syncing Notes Across Devices**:
   - Google Keep automatically syncs your notes across all devices connected to your Google account. This means that any notes you create on your phone, tablet, or computer will be available to you no matter where you are.

Chapter 9: Advanced Features

Google Drive offers a variety of advanced features that can enhance your file management and collaboration capabilities. In this chapter, we'll dive into Shared Drives, how to work with file versions, and how to use add-ons to integrate third-party tools into Google Drive.

1. Shared Drives

Shared Drives (formerly called Team Drives) allow teams and organizations to store and collaborate on files more effectively. Files in a Shared Drive are owned by the team, not an individual, and are accessible by all members of the drive.

What are Shared Drives?

Shared Drives are a feature of Google Drive designed for teams. Unlike regular Google Drive folders, Shared Drives allow multiple users to access and manage files with predefined permissions, without worrying about who owns the file. This makes it ideal for businesses, projects, or any collaborative environment.

- **Ownership**: Files in Shared Drives are owned by the team rather than an individual. This means that the files stay with the organization even if someone leaves.
- **Access Control**: You can manage who can view, comment, edit, or manage files in a Shared Drive, giving you more granular control over team collaboration.

- **File Accessibility**: All members of the Shared Drive have access to all the files within it, and new members can be added as needed.

Setting Up and Managing a Shared Drive

1. **Creating a New Shared Drive**:
   - Open **Google Drive** in your browser.
   - On the left-hand side, click on **Shared Drives**.
   - Click the **+ New** button at the top-left corner to create a new Shared Drive.
   - Give your Shared Drive a name and click **Create**.

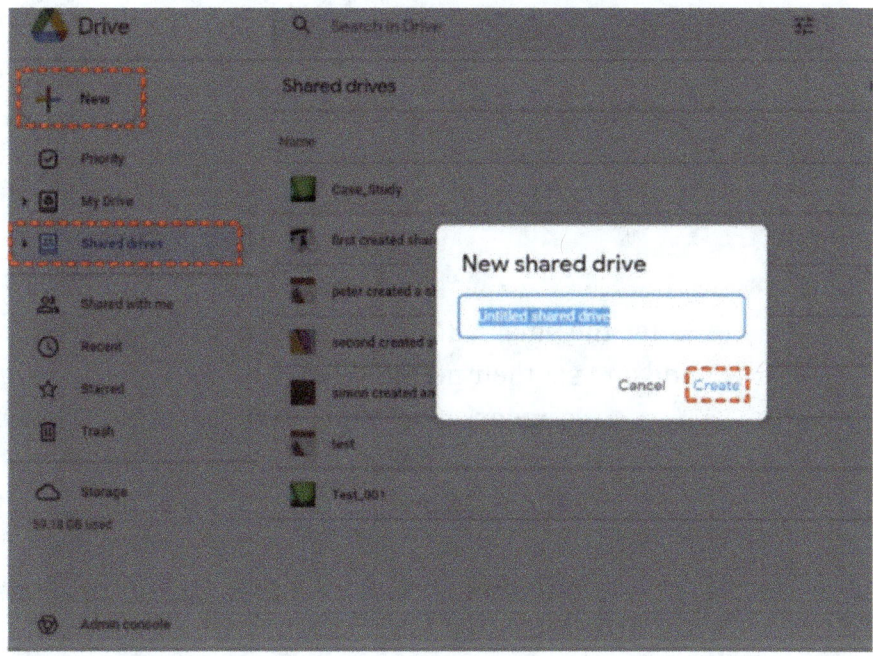

2. **Adding Members and Setting Permissions**:

- After creating the Shared Drive, click on the name of the drive to open it.
- At the top, click **Manage Members**.

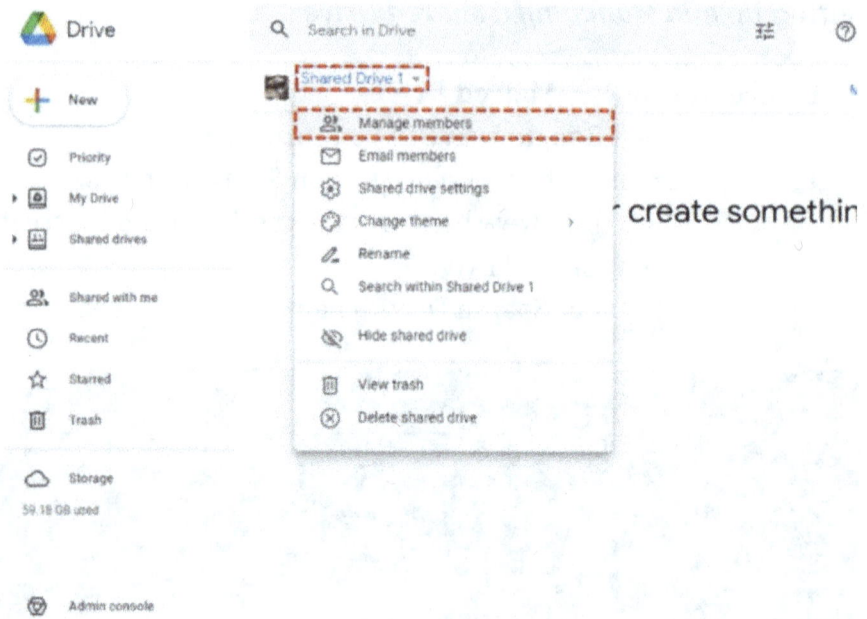

- Enter the email addresses of the people you want to add and set their permissions:
  - **Manager**: Can add, remove, and manage members and files.
  - **Content Manager**: Can manage content but not members.
  - **Contributor**: Can edit files but not manage files or members.
  - **Commenter**: Can comment on files but not edit them.
  - **Viewer**: Can only view files.

○ Click **Send** to invite members.

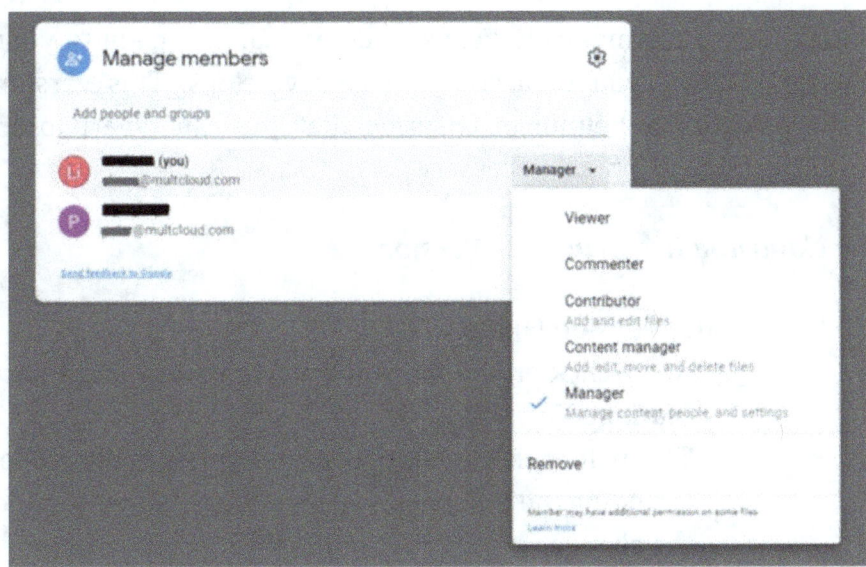

3. **Organizing and Managing Files in Shared Drives**:
   ○ Files in Shared Drives can be organized into folders just like in your personal Drive.
   ○ Drag and drop files into Shared Drive folders.
   ○ You can manage the files by clicking on them and choosing from various options like moving, renaming, and deleting.

4. **Sharing Files in Shared Drives**:
   ○ Any file added to the Shared Drive is automatically shared with all members.
   ○ You can change the sharing settings on individual files if needed by right-clicking and selecting **Share**. Choose who can access the file and set permissions.

2. File Versions

Google Drive automatically keeps track of changes made to your files and allows you to access previous versions. This version history feature is helpful in ensuring that you can revert to an earlier version of a file if necessary.

Checking and Restoring File Versions

1. **Viewing Version History**:
   - Right-click on the file you want to review and select **Manage Versions**.
   - This will open a list of all previous versions of the file, including the time it was last modified and who made the changes.
   - You can see the file's name, size, and the version number. Versions are automatically saved each time a file is edited.
2. **Restoring a Previous Version**:
   - In the **Manage Versions** window, click on the version you wish to restore.
   - Select **Restore** to revert to that version of the file. The restored version will be the active file, but you can always go back to another version if needed.
3. **Renaming Versions**:
   - You can also rename a version for better organization. Click on the version and choose **Rename** to give it a more descriptive name.
4. **Downloading Previous Versions**:
   - If you need to keep a record of previous versions, click **Download** next to the version you want to save.

This will download a copy of that version to your computer.

Version Control Best Practices:

- Make sure to use version history regularly, especially for collaborative projects, as this allows you to track who made what changes.
- Communicate with team members about the importance of naming versions or leaving comments for better version tracking.

3. Using Add-ons

Add-ons are third-party tools that enhance the functionality of Google Drive by adding new features, integrations, or capabilities. These tools can help you streamline your workflow, improve collaboration, and automate repetitive tasks.

Enhancing Drive Functionality with Third-Party Tools

1. **Installing Add-ons**:
    - Open a Google Workspace app like Google Docs or Google Sheets.
    - Click on **Add-ons** in the top menu, then select **Get add-ons**. This will open the Google Workspace Marketplace.

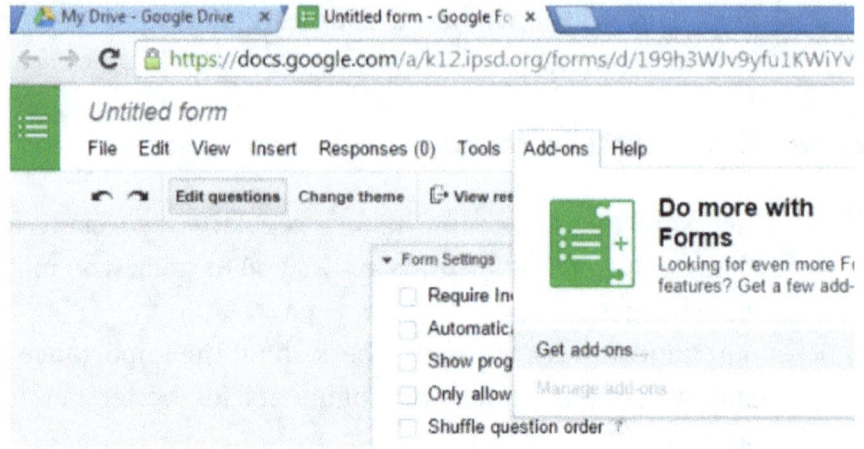

- o Browse or search for the add-on you want to install, then click **Install**.
- o Follow the on-screen prompts to grant the necessary permissions and complete the installation.

2. **Using Add-ons**:
   - o Once the add-on is installed, you can access it by going back to the **Add-ons** menu in the Google Workspace app.
   - o From there, you can select the add-on you installed and use its features to improve your productivity.
   - o Some add-ons may require you to sign in to an external account or configure specific settings to integrate them into your workflow.

3. **Popular Add-ons for Google Drive**:
   - o **DocuSign**: Allows you to sign and send documents directly from Google Docs.
   - o **Lucidchart Diagrams**: Integrates with Google Drive to create flowcharts, mind maps, and diagrams.

- o **Google Forms Add-ons**: Enhance your forms with extra features, such as automated workflows, additional question types, or improved data analysis.
- o **HelloSign**: Allows you to request signatures for documents stored in Google Drive.

4. **Managing Add-ons**:
   - o To remove an add-on, go to **Add-ons** > **Manage add-ons** and select the add-on you want to remove.
   - o You can also disable add-ons temporarily if you don't need them, which helps keep your workspace uncluttered.

Chapter 10: Security and Privacy

Google Drive provides powerful tools to help protect the privacy of your files and secure your account. In this chapter, we'll explore how to manage file privacy settings, enhance account security, and follow best practices for secure sharing to keep your data safe.

1. File Privacy Settings

Google Drive allows you to set specific privacy levels for each file and folder you store, helping you control who can access your content and how they can interact with it.

Controlling Who Can View, Edit, or Share Files

1. **Changing Sharing Settings for a File or Folder**:
   - Right-click on the file or folder you want to adjust privacy settings for.
   - Select **Share** from the context menu.
   - In the **Share with People and Groups** window, you'll see a list of people who have access to the file or folder.
   - Click the **pencil icon** next to each person's name to adjust their permissions:
     - **Viewer**: Can only view the file.
     - **Commenter**: Can view and add comments to the file but cannot edit it.
     - **Editor**: Can make changes to the file, add or remove content, and share the file with others.

- To add a new person, enter their email address in the **Add People and Groups** field and assign a role (Viewer, Commenter, or Editor).

2. **Changing Link Sharing Settings**:
   - If the file or folder is shared via a link, you can control who can access it by clicking on **Get Link**.
   - Under the link-sharing options, select the appropriate setting:
     - **Restricted**: Only people explicitly added can access the file.
     - **Anyone with the link**: Anyone who has the link can access the file (select the appropriate role: Viewer, Commenter, or Editor).
   - You can also disable link sharing at any time by selecting **Turn off link sharing**.

3. **Preventing File Sharing**:
   - If you don't want others to share a file further, click on the **gear icon** in the top-right corner of the **Share with People and Groups** window.

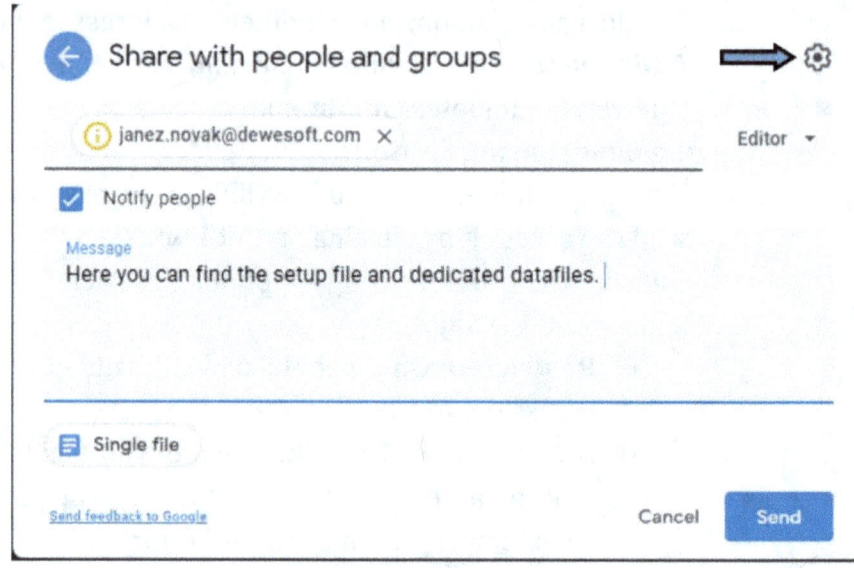

- o Uncheck the option **Editors can change permissions and share**.
- o This setting ensures only the owner can change sharing permissions and prevent anyone else from sharing the file with others.

2. Account Security

Ensuring the security of your Google account is crucial, as it holds all your data and personal information. By taking extra steps to secure your account, you minimize the risk of unauthorized access.

Enabling Two-Factor Authentication (2FA)

Two-factor authentication (2FA) adds an additional layer of security by requiring a second verification step, usually via your mobile phone, in addition to your password.

1. **Setting up 2FA**:
    o Go to your Google Account settings by visiting myaccount.google.com.
    o In the **Security** tab, click on **2-Step Verification**.
    o Click **Get Started** and follow the instructions to link your mobile phone number to your account.
    o Google will send you a verification code to your phone to complete the setup.

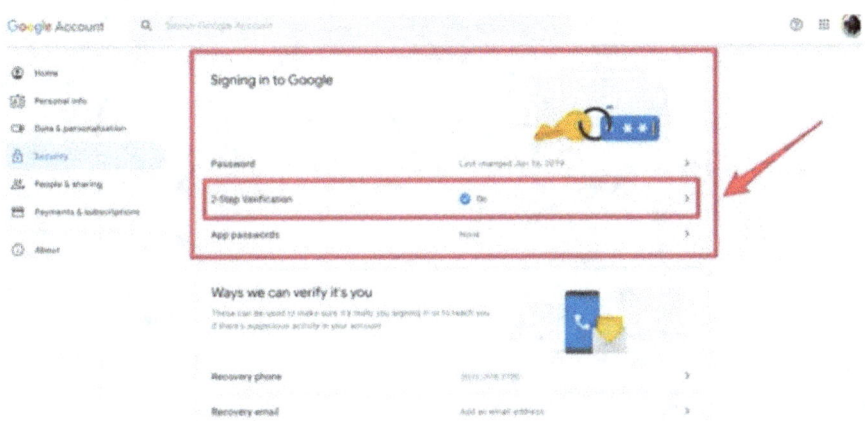

2. **Choosing Your 2FA Method**:
    o **Google prompts**: When you sign in, Google will send you a prompt on your phone asking if you're trying to log in.
    o **Authenticator app**: Use an app like Google Authenticator or Authy to generate a time-based one-time password (TOTP).
    o **SMS or voice call**: Google will send a verification code to your phone via text message or call.

- Security key: For the highest level of security, you can use a physical security key (such as a USB device or Bluetooth key) to authenticate.

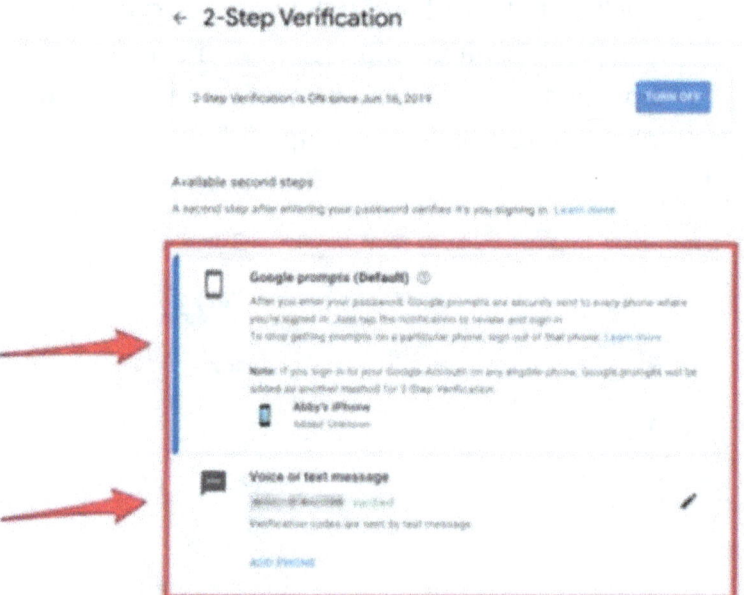

3. **Verifying Your Backup Options:**
   - Google also offers backup options, such as recovery codes or a secondary phone number, to ensure you can access your account if you lose access to your primary verification method.
4. **Turning Off 2FA (if needed):**
   - If you decide to disable 2FA, return to the **Security** tab of your Google Account settings and select **2-Step Verification**. Click **Turn off** and follow the instructions.

Managing Connected Apps and Devices

Google Drive works seamlessly with a wide range of apps and devices. However, it's important to regularly check and manage the apps and devices that are connected to your Google account to maintain security.

1. **Managing Connected Apps**:
   - Go to your **Google Account settings** and click on the **Security** tab.
   - Scroll down to **Third-party apps with account access** and click **Manage third-party access**.
   - Here, you can see which apps and websites have access to your Google account and what level of access they have (e.g., viewing email, managing files in Google Drive).
   - If you see any suspicious or unfamiliar apps, click on them and select **Remove Access** to disconnect them from your Google account.
2. **Managing Devices**:
   - In the **Security** tab, under **Your Devices**, you'll see a list of all devices that have recently accessed your Google Account.
   - Review the list and remove any devices you don't recognize by clicking **Remove** next to the device.
   - If you suspect unauthorized access, you can also **sign out of all devices** from this page.

3. Tips for Secure Sharing

Sharing files securely is essential, especially when handling sensitive or personal information. By following the right practices, you can ensure that your data stays protected while collaborating with others.

Protecting Sensitive Data with Advanced Settings

1. **Restricting Download, Print, and Copy Options**:
   - When sharing files with others, especially if they contain sensitive information, you can restrict the ability for others to download, print, or copy the file.
   - In the **Share with People and Groups** window, click on the **gear icon** and uncheck **Viewers and Commenters can see the option to download, print, and copy**.
   - This prevents recipients from downloading or sharing the file's content.
2. **Using Expiration Dates for Shared Links**:
   - Google Drive allows you to set expiration dates for shared links. This ensures that the link will no longer work after a certain time, adding another layer of security.
   - To do this, click on the **Get Link** section and select **Link settings**.
   - Under the **Expiration date** option, set a date when the link will expire.
3. **Using Google Vault (for Businesses)**:

- o If you're using Google Drive through a G Suite (Google Workspace) account, Google Vault is a tool for archiving and managing data retention.
- o Vault allows you to set retention rules for files, ensuring that they are automatically deleted or archived according to company policies.
- o Vault also allows you to set eDiscovery settings, allowing administrators to search and manage files that may be under investigation or subject to legal holds.

4. **Enabling Virus Scan for Uploaded Files**:
   - o Google Drive automatically scans files for viruses upon upload, but it's a good idea to double-check that your organization's policies are in place for enhanced security.
   - o Always be cautious about downloading or sharing files from unknown sources, even if they've been scanned by Google.

Chapter 11: Google Drive for Mobile

Google Drive's mobile app is designed to offer a seamless experience when accessing, uploading, and managing your files on the go. This chapter explores the mobile app's features, including how it differs from the desktop version, how to scan documents directly with your phone's camera, and the mobile-specific features that make it a versatile tool.

1. Overview of the Mobile App

The Google Drive mobile app is available for both iOS and Android devices and offers a more streamlined experience compared to the desktop version. While it provides similar core functionalities, there are some key differences to be aware of when using the app on your phone or tablet.

Key Differences from the Desktop Version

- **Simplified Interface**: The mobile app offers a simplified interface, with a focus on essential features for quick access and management. It's optimized for smaller screens and uses touch gestures for navigation.
- **Limited File Management**: While the mobile app allows you to manage and organize your files, some advanced features—like file syncing and detailed folder organization—are more accessible from the desktop version.

- **Accessing Files**: On mobile, your files are automatically synced as long as you have an internet connection. You can also access files offline if you enable the offline mode (covered later).
- **Drag-and-Drop**: Unlike the desktop version where drag-and-drop is used to move files, on mobile, you need to use the file options to move or organize files within the app.

2. Scanning Documents

The Google Drive mobile app allows you to scan physical documents using your phone's camera. This feature is particularly useful for quickly digitizing paper documents, receipts, or notes directly into your Google Drive.

Using Your Phone's Camera to Scan and Upload

1. **Opening the Camera Scan**:
   o Open the Google Drive app on your phone.
   o Tap the **+** (plus) button located at the bottom right of the screen.
   o From the options, select **Scan**. This will open your phone's camera for scanning.
2. **Scanning the Document**:
   o Place the document or image you want to scan on a flat surface.
   o Align the document within the camera frame and ensure it's clear and legible.
   o Tap the **Shutter button** to capture the scan. The app will automatically crop and enhance the scan for better readability.

3. **Saving the Scanned Document**:
   - After scanning, you can review the document. If needed, adjust the edges of the scan or retake it.
   - Once satisfied with the scan, tap **Save**. You will be prompted to name the file and select its destination folder within Google Drive.
   - The scanned document is now available as a PDF file in your Drive, ready for sharing, editing, or organizing.

3. Mobile-Specific Features

The mobile app offers some unique features that help enhance your productivity while on the go. These features are especially helpful for users who need quick access to files, collaboration, or offline access while traveling or working in areas with limited internet.

Using Offline Mode

Offline mode is a key feature for mobile users who need to access and work on their files without a stable internet connection. With offline mode enabled, Google Drive allows you to access, edit, and even create new files, all without an internet connection.

1. **Enabling Offline Mode**:
   - Open the Google Drive app on your mobile device.
   - Locate the file or folder you want to make available offline.
   - Tap on the **three-dot menu** next to the file or folder.

- o Select **Available Offline** from the menu. The file will be downloaded to your device and available for offline access.
2. **Editing Files Offline**:
     - o Once a file is available offline, you can open and edit it just as you would with an internet connection. Any changes made will be saved locally on your device.
     - o When you reconnect to the internet, your changes will automatically sync with your Google Drive, ensuring that your online storage is updated.
3. **Managing Offline Files**:
     - o To manage offline files, go to the **Offline** section in the Drive app. Here, you can see which files are available offline and remove them when they're no longer needed to free up storage space.

Sharing on the Go

The mobile app makes it easy to share files and collaborate while you're away from your computer. Whether you're on a business trip or meeting friends, sharing documents is just a tap away.

1. **Sharing Files**:
     - o To share a file, tap the **three-dot menu** next to the file.
     - o Select **Share** to send the file to others via email, or select **Copy Link** to share the file through messaging apps, social media, etc.
2. **Sharing Files from Other Apps**:
     - o The Google Drive mobile app integrates with your device's other apps, making it easy to share files from

within other apps (e.g., from photos, email, or document editors).

- o Open the file you want to share in another app, and select the **Share** button. Choose Google Drive from the list of sharing options.

3. **Collaborating on Files**:
   - o Real-time collaboration on documents is available through the Google Docs, Sheets, and Slides apps, which are integrated with Google Drive.
   - o You can see changes made by other collaborators instantly and add your own comments or suggestions while on the go.

Chapter 12: Integrations with Third-Party Apps

Google Drive offers a variety of integrations with third-party apps that help extend its functionality and improve your productivity. From adding custom tools to integrating with popular Microsoft Office apps, and automating repetitive workflows, these integrations allow you to streamline your work processes and access more powerful features within Google Drive. This chapter explores these integrations in detail.

1. Google Workspace Marketplace

The **Google Workspace Marketplace** provides a wide range of third-party apps that integrate seamlessly with Google Drive. These apps can enhance your workflow, offering tools for project management, document signing, time tracking, and much more. Let's walk through how you can install, manage, and use these apps in Google Drive.

Installing and Managing Apps

1. **Opening the Google Workspace Marketplace**:
   - Open Google Drive in your browser.
   - In the upper-right corner, click on the **gear icon** (settings) and select **Get add-ons**. This will take you to the Google Workspace Marketplace.
2. **Searching for Apps**:

- Use the search bar at the top of the Marketplace to find the app you want to integrate with Google Drive.
- You can also browse categories like **Project Management**, **Business Tools**, or **Productivity** to find apps that match your needs.

3. **Installing an App**:
   - Once you've found the app, click on it to view more details.
   - Click the **Install** button, and you may need to grant the app permission to access your Google Drive files.
   - Follow the prompts to complete the installation process. The app will now be available within Google Drive or other Google Workspace tools like Docs, Sheets, or Slides.

4. **Managing Installed Apps**:
   - To manage your installed apps, return to the Google Workspace Marketplace and click on **Manage Apps** from the menu on the left.
   - Here, you can enable, disable, or uninstall any apps you've installed. If you no longer need an app or want to update it, you can easily do so from this page.

5. **Using Integrated Apps**:
   - After installing an app, you can access it directly from within Google Drive or other Google Workspace tools. For example, you may see a new option in the **Add-ons** menu within Google Docs or Sheets.
   - Some apps allow you to use advanced tools, like digital signatures in **DocuSign** or file organization in **Trello**, right from within Google Drive.

2. Integration with Microsoft Office

Google Drive offers robust integration with **Microsoft Office** products, such as Word, Excel, and PowerPoint. This allows you to store, view, and even edit Microsoft Office files directly within Google Drive without needing to open Microsoft Office programs. Whether you're working with colleagues who use Microsoft Office or prefer Office tools, this integration makes it easy to switch between Google and Microsoft ecosystems.

Editing Word and Excel Files in Drive

1. **Uploading Microsoft Office Files**:
   - o To store a Word or Excel file in Google Drive, simply drag and drop the file into your Drive. Alternatively, use the **New** button in Drive and select **File upload** to choose files from your computer.
   - o Google Drive automatically recognizes these files and allows you to view and edit them.
2. **Viewing Office Files**:
   - o When you open a Word or Excel file in Google Drive, it will be displayed in **Google Docs** or **Google Sheets** in **view-only mode** by default.
   - o To make edits, you can convert the file into a Google Docs or Sheets file, but keep in mind that the formatting might change during conversion.
3. **Editing Office Files**:
   - o To edit a Microsoft Word or Excel file without converting it, you can use the **Google Drive File Stream** (for desktop users) or use Google's **Quickoffice Editor** integration. These allow you to

open and edit Office files without converting them to Google formats.

4. **Collaborating on Office Files**:
    - Google Drive allows multiple users to collaborate on Microsoft Office files in real-time, just like Google Docs or Sheets. You can comment on files, track changes, and leave suggestions.

5. **Saving Changes**:
    - When you edit an Office file, changes are saved directly to your Google Drive. You can choose whether to keep the file in its original format (Word or Excel) or save a copy in Google Docs or Sheets format for easier collaboration with other Google users.

3. Automating Workflows

One of the most powerful ways to enhance your productivity with Google Drive is by automating repetitive tasks using third-party tools like **Zapier**. Zapier connects Google Drive with hundreds of apps, enabling you to automate workflows that would normally require manual effort. Whether you're automatically saving email attachments to Drive, backing up files, or syncing documents between apps, Zapier helps streamline your processes.

Using Tools Like Zapier to Automate Repetitive Tasks

1. **Creating a Zapier Account**:
    - To get started with automation, you'll need a Zapier account. Go to zapier.com and sign up for a free account.

2. **Connecting Google Drive to Zapier**:
    - After signing up, you can connect your Google Drive account to Zapier by selecting **Google Drive** from the list of apps.
    - Follow the on-screen instructions to authenticate your Google Drive account with Zapier.
3. **Creating a Zap (Automation Task)**:
    - A **Zap** is an automation workflow that connects two apps. To create one, click on the **Make a Zap** button on your Zapier dashboard.
    - Choose a **trigger** app (for example, Gmail) and set up the conditions (such as when a new email with an attachment is received).
    - Next, choose Google Drive as the **action** app and define what should happen when the trigger is activated (e.g., save the email attachment to a specific folder in Google Drive).
4. **Examples of Automations**:
    - **Automatically Upload Email Attachments**: Set up a Zap to automatically save email attachments from Gmail to a designated folder in Google Drive.
    - **Create Google Docs from New Entries in a Form**: Use a Zap to create a new Google Doc each time a user submits a form (e.g., Google Forms or Typeform).
    - **Sync Google Drive with Dropbox**: Automate the process of backing up files in Google Drive to Dropbox, keeping all files synced between the two platforms.
5. **Managing Zaps**:
    - After creating your Zaps, you can manage them from your Zapier dashboard. Turn Zaps on or off, view

their activity logs, or modify the triggers and actions as needed.

Chapter 13: Troubleshooting Common Issues

Despite its simplicity and ease of use, Google Drive users may occasionally encounter issues ranging from storage problems to file upload failures. This chapter will help you troubleshoot and resolve some of the most common issues you may face when using Google Drive. Whether it's freeing up space, fixing syncing issues, or dealing with upload errors, this guide will walk you through the solutions step by step.

1. Storage Management

As you upload files to Google Drive, you may eventually run into storage limitations. If you're using the free plan, which includes 15 GB of storage, you might need to manage your space to avoid hitting the limit. Here's how you can free up space and manage your Google Drive storage efficiently.

Freeing Up Space in Drive

1. **Check Your Storage Usage**:
   - To see how much storage you've used, go to Google Drive and click on the **Storage** link at the bottom left of the screen. This will show a breakdown of your usage across Google Drive, Gmail, and Google Photos.
2. **Delete Unnecessary Files**:
   - Review your files and delete those you no longer need. To delete a file, right-click on it and select

Remove. Remember that deleted files are moved to the Trash and still count against your storage until permanently deleted.

- o To empty the Trash, go to the **Trash** section in Google Drive, click **Empty Trash**, and confirm.

3. **Delete Large Files**:
   - o If you're running low on storage, finding and removing large files can free up significant space. Click on **Storage** in the left sidebar to see files sorted by size, and delete any large, unnecessary ones.

4. **Transfer Files to External Storage**:
   - o If you have files you don't need immediate access to but want to keep, consider downloading them to an external hard drive or using another cloud storage service.

Identifying and Removing Large Files

1. **Using Storage Insights**:
   - o In Google Drive, navigate to the **Storage** section (left-hand sidebar) to see a list of your largest files.
   - o Sort your files by size to quickly identify which ones are taking up the most space.

2. **Remove or Move Large Files**:
   - o Once identified, you can either delete or transfer large files to another storage solution. If you're using Google Photos or Gmail, these files also contribute to your storage, so check them if you're low on space.

2. Sync Errors

Sync issues can occur when the Google Drive desktop app fails to sync files correctly. This can happen for various reasons, such as an unstable internet connection, conflicting software, or settings that need adjustment. Here's how you can resolve these syncing problems on both desktop and mobile.

Resolving Syncing Problems on Desktop and Mobile

1. **Check Your Internet Connection**:
   o A stable internet connection is essential for syncing. Make sure you're connected to the internet and that there are no issues with your connection.
2. **Restart Google Drive**:
   o Sometimes, simply restarting the Google Drive desktop app can solve sync issues. Close the app and reopen it to see if syncing resumes correctly.
3. **Check File Sync Status**:
   o Open the Google Drive app on your desktop and look for the sync status icon (a circular arrow). If the icon is spinning or showing an error symbol, there is an issue.
   o Right-click on the icon and select **View sync status** to see which files are pending or have encountered errors.
4. **Update Google Drive**:
   o Ensure that you are using the latest version of the Google Drive app. Outdated versions may cause sync problems. Go to the app store (for mobile) or download the latest version from the Google website for desktop.
5. **Check for Conflicting Files**:

- If syncing is paused or fails for specific files, check for any file conflicts. Google Drive may fail to sync if a file is open in another program, or if there are permission issues. Close conflicting apps or adjust permissions if necessary.

6. **Reinstall Google Drive**:
   - If none of the above steps work, try uninstalling and reinstalling the Google Drive app. This often resolves any deeper issues that might be causing sync problems.

7. **Syncing on Mobile**:
   - For mobile devices, go to the Google Drive app and tap the **Menu** (three horizontal lines in the upper left). Scroll down to **Settings** and tap **Offline**. Ensure that the "Offline mode" is enabled if you need to access files offline.

8. **Mobile Syncing Issues**:
   - If files aren't syncing on your mobile device, ensure that your device is connected to Wi-Fi and not consuming too much data. If you're using cellular data, ensure the setting for syncing over mobile data is enabled in your Drive app settings.

3. File Upload Problems

File upload failures are common, and several factors can prevent files from uploading correctly to Google Drive. These might include file size, internet connectivity, or compatibility issues. Below are some solutions to help you troubleshoot and resolve upload issues.

Solutions for Failed or Incomplete Uploads

1. **Check File Size Limits**:
   - o Google Drive has a file size limit for uploads. You can upload files up to **5 TB** in size, provided you have enough storage space. If your file exceeds this limit, you will need to reduce its size or split it into smaller parts.

2. **Check Your Internet Connection**:
   - o A slow or intermittent internet connection can cause uploads to fail. Ensure that your connection is stable and that you're not experiencing any interruptions. You can check your connection speed using a speed test website.

3. **Clear Your Browser's Cache**:
   - o If you're uploading files through your browser and the upload fails, clear your browser's cache. Overloaded cache files can cause issues with uploading. To do this, go to your browser's settings and clear browsing data.

4. **Try a Different Browser or Device**:
   - o Sometimes, the issue may be related to the browser or device you are using. Try uploading your file on a different browser or device to rule out browser-related problems.

5. **Pause and Resume Upload**:
   - o If an upload is stuck or incomplete, try pausing it and then resuming. On the desktop, click on the Google Drive icon, go to **View sync status**, and click **Pause** or **Resume** for the specific file.

6. **Disable Browser Extensions**:

- o Certain browser extensions (such as ad-blockers) may interfere with the upload process. Disable any non-essential extensions and try uploading the file again.

7. **Re-upload the File**:
   - o If all else fails, try deleting the failed upload and uploading the file again. You may also try uploading a smaller portion of the file (if applicable) to check if the issue lies with the file itself.

Chapter 14: Tips and Tricks for Beginners

Google Drive is not just for storing files; it's a versatile tool that can help boost productivity, streamline workflows, and even assist with creative tasks. In this chapter, we will explore some helpful tips and tricks that will make using Google Drive even more efficient, whether you're managing projects, organizing personal files, or discovering creative uses for the platform.

1. Keyboard Shortcuts

Google Drive has a variety of keyboard shortcuts that can save you time and improve your productivity. By mastering these shortcuts, you'll be able to navigate through Drive faster and perform common tasks with ease.

Popular Shortcuts to Boost Productivity

1. **Navigation Shortcuts**:
    - **Go to the Search bar: Ctrl + /** (Windows) or **Cmd + /** (Mac)
    - **Open the "My Drive" view: G + D**
    - **Open the Shared with Me view: G + S**
    - **Go to the Trash: G + T**
    - **Go to the Recent view: G + R**
2. **File and Folder Shortcuts**:
    - **Create a new document: Shift + T**
    - **Create a new spreadsheet: Shift + S**

- Create a new presentation: **Shift + P**
- Create a new folder: **Shift + F**
- Open a file: **Enter**
- Rename a file: **N**
- Move a file: **Z**

3. **Viewing and Editing Shortcuts**:
   - **Select multiple files: Ctrl + click** (Windows) or **Cmd + click** (Mac)
   - **Toggle between list and grid view: Ctrl + Alt + 1** (list view), **Ctrl + Alt + 2** (grid view)
   - **Zoom in/out on a file: Ctrl + +** (zoom in) / **Ctrl + -** (zoom out) on Windows, **Cmd + + / Cmd + -** on Mac
   - **Undo action: Ctrl + Z** (Windows) or **Cmd + Z** (Mac)
   - **Redo action: Ctrl + Y** (Windows) or **Cmd + Shift + Z** (Mac)

These shortcuts can save you significant time when navigating through Google Drive and performing routine tasks. Once you become familiar with them, you'll notice a marked increase in your efficiency.

2. Productivity Tips

Google Drive isn't just a file storage service; it can also be used as a powerful tool for managing projects and organizing your daily tasks. With a few simple strategies, you can optimize your workflow and make Google Drive a central hub for your work.

Using Drive for Project Management

1. **Organize Files into Project Folders**:

- Create a separate folder for each project you are working on. Inside the folder, you can store all relevant documents, spreadsheets, presentations, and images. This keeps everything organized and makes it easy to find what you need.

2. **Collaborate on Documents**:
   - Use Google Docs, Sheets, and Slides for real-time collaboration. You can invite team members to edit documents, leave comments, and suggest changes. This makes working on projects as a team more efficient and transparent.

3. **Use Google Keep for Notes**:
   - Google Keep integrates with Google Drive and can be used for taking quick notes, making to-do lists, or saving reminders. You can easily add these notes to your project folders for reference.

4. **Use Google Calendar for Deadlines**:
   - Sync Google Drive with Google Calendar to keep track of project deadlines. You can attach files to calendar events to make sure everything is organized in one place.

5. **Create Templates for Repetitive Tasks**:
   - For recurring projects or tasks, create document templates that can be quickly customized. For example, if you often create reports, set up a Google Docs template with predefined sections and formatting.

Setting Up Daily Workflows with Drive

1. **Centralized File Storage**:

- Store all your work-related files in Google Drive and use folders to organize them by project, client, or category. This allows you to quickly find files as you go about your daily tasks.

2. **Use Google Sheets for Task Management**:
   - Set up a simple task tracking system using Google Sheets. Create columns for task name, due date, priority, and completion status. This can serve as a daily to-do list to keep track of what you need to accomplish.

3. **Sync Your Files Across Devices**:
   - Enable Google Drive syncing on both your desktop and mobile devices so that you can access your files anytime, anywhere. This ensures that you're never without your work, even when you're on the go.

4. **Set Up Alerts for File Updates**:
   - If you're working on shared files, set up notifications to alert you whenever changes are made. This way, you'll always be aware of new updates and avoid missing important information.

3. Creative Uses of Google Drive

Google Drive isn't just for work-related tasks. Its versatility allows for creative uses, making it an excellent tool for personal organization, journaling, and more. Here are some ideas to get you started:

Using Drive for Journaling, Budgeting, and Organizing Personal Files

1. **Journaling**:
   o Use Google Docs to create a digital journal. You can write daily entries, add images, and even voice memos. Create separate folders for different years or topics, making it easy to look back on past entries.
2. **Budgeting**:
   o Google Sheets can be an excellent tool for tracking your finances. Create a budgeting spreadsheet with columns for income, expenses, and savings. Use formulas to automatically calculate totals and track your financial progress over time.
3. **Organizing Personal Files**:
   o Google Drive is an excellent place to store and organize personal documents such as tax forms, receipts, and important personal records. Create a folder structure that works for you and store files like scanned documents or contracts for easy access.
4. **Creative Writing**:
   o If you're a writer, Google Drive can be a great tool to store your stories, poetry, or manuscripts. You can even share your drafts with others for feedback and make collaborative edits in real-time.
5. **Photo Storage and Organization**:
   o Store your personal photos and videos in Google Drive. You can organize them into albums or by event, making it easy to access your memories whenever you need them. With Google Photos integration, you can also take advantage of automatic photo backups.

6. **Planning and Organizing Events**:
    - If you're planning a special event, such as a wedding or party, you can use Google Drive to store important files like guest lists, invitations, and venue details. Collaborate with others by sharing these files for real-time updates and contributions.

Chapter 15: Best Practices and Conclusion

In this final chapter, we'll wrap up everything you've learned about Google Drive, focusing on the best practices for getting the most out of the platform. You'll also find some encouragement to explore its advanced features, answers to common questions, and a roadmap for your next steps as you continue using Google Drive for all your personal and professional needs.

1. Top 10 Tips for Mastering Google Drive

To truly master Google Drive and make the most out of its vast array of features, here are the top 10 tips that will help you work smarter and stay organized:

1. **Organize with Folders:**
    o   Keep your Drive clutter-free by organizing files into clearly labeled folders. This simple habit will save you time in the long run.
2. **Use Search Filters:**
    o   Take advantage of Google Drive's search bar and advanced filters to quickly locate files, especially when dealing with a large number of documents.
3. **Sync for Access Anywhere:**
    o   Enable syncing on your desktop and mobile devices to ensure you have access to your files no matter where you are.

4. **Collaborate in Real-Time**:
    o Use Google Docs, Sheets, and Slides to collaborate with others on projects. Real-time editing and commenting help improve team productivity.
5. **Keep Files Secure**:
    o Review your file and folder permissions regularly to ensure only the right people have access to your files. Enable two-factor authentication for added security.
6. **Use Keyboard Shortcuts**:
    o Speed up your workflow by learning keyboard shortcuts. These will help you navigate Google Drive and perform tasks much faster.
7. **Use the Mobile App**:
    o Download the Google Drive mobile app so you can access and edit files on the go. This is especially useful for remote work or managing files while traveling.
8. **Take Advantage of Google Keep**:
    o Use Google Keep to take quick notes or create to-do lists, and link them to your Drive files for easy reference.
9. **Manage Storage Space**:
    o Regularly check your storage usage and remove or archive old files you no longer need. Google Drive offers free storage up to a certain limit, and it's easy to run out of space.
10. **Enable Offline Mode**:
    o Set up offline mode for essential files. This allows you to continue working even when you don't have an internet connection.

By following these tips, you'll become much more efficient in using Google Drive and get the most value from it.

2. Encouragement for Exploring Advanced Features

While you've learned a lot about the basics of Google Drive, there are plenty of advanced features that can help you further optimize your experience and enhance your workflows. Here are some areas to explore:

- **Shared Drives**:
  - If you're working with a team or group, explore Shared Drives. These allow you to create central spaces where files are automatically accessible to all members, without worrying about sharing permissions.
- **Google Apps Integration**:
  - Learn to integrate Google Drive with other Google Workspace apps, such as Google Calendar, Google Keep, and Google Photos, to make your workflow even more seamless.
- **Zapier Automation**:
  - Automate tasks between Google Drive and other third-party apps using tools like Zapier. This can save you time on repetitive actions, such as automatically saving email attachments to Drive or syncing data between apps.
- **File Version Control**:
  - Take advantage of Google Drive's version history to track changes and restore previous versions of your

files. This is particularly useful when working on documents or spreadsheets over time.

- **Google Workspace Marketplace**:
    - ○ Browse the Google Workspace Marketplace to discover add-ons and integrations that can extend Google Drive's capabilities. Whether it's project management tools, document signing, or image editing, there's likely an add-on for it.

Exploring these advanced features will not only improve your productivity but also help you unlock the full potential of Google Drive.

3. FAQs

Just in case you jumped straight to this section to quickly solve an issue, here are some common questions you might have as you continue your journey with Google Drive:

Q1: Can I use Google Drive without an internet connection?
A1: Yes! You can enable offline mode in Google Drive, allowing you to view and edit your files without an internet connection. Changes will sync when you reconnect to the internet.

Q2: How can I recover a deleted file?
A2: Files deleted from Google Drive go to the Trash. You can restore files from the Trash unless they have been permanently deleted (after 30 days).

Q3: Can I password-protect files in Google Drive?
A3: Google Drive does not have a built-in feature to password-

protect individual files. However, you can restrict access to specific users by adjusting the file's sharing permissions.

Q4: What's the difference between Google Drive and Google One?

A4: Google Drive is the cloud storage service itself, while Google One is a subscription service that offers expanded storage, family sharing, and other perks. Google One is a paid plan that increases your storage capacity beyond the free limit.

Q5: How can I automate tasks in Google Drive?

A5: You can automate tasks in Google Drive using third-party tools like Zapier. These tools allow you to set up automatic workflows, such as saving attachments from Gmail directly to Drive.

Appendices

These appendices provide additional resources to help you with your Google Drive experience. Whether you're looking for a quick reference to important terms or need a cheat sheet to get started, these sections will guide you in your Google Drive journey.

Glossary of Terms

Here's a quick reference guide for some of the most commonly used terms related to Google Drive. Understanding these terms will help you navigate Google Drive with ease.

- **Google Drive**: Google's cloud storage service where you can store, access, and share files online.
- **Google Workspace**: A suite of productivity tools including Google Docs, Sheets, Slides, Gmail, and more, which integrates seamlessly with Google Drive.
- **File Version History**: A feature in Google Drive that allows you to view and revert to previous versions of a file, making it easy to track changes and undo mistakes.
- **Shared Drive**: A collaborative space within Google Drive that allows multiple people to access and contribute to files and folders. Unlike "My Drive," files in a Shared Drive are owned by the team or organization rather than an individual.
- **Offline Mode**: A feature that lets you access and edit files stored in Google Drive even when you don't have an internet

connection. Any changes made offline are synced once you're back online.

- **Permission Levels**: The access rights given to users when sharing files in Google Drive. The main permission levels are:
  - o **Viewer**: Can only view the file.
  - o **Commenter**: Can view and leave comments on the file.
  - o **Editor**: Can edit the file.
- **Google Keep**: A note-taking app integrated with Google Drive that allows you to create quick notes, to-do lists, and reminders.
- **Trash**: A folder in Google Drive where deleted files are temporarily stored. You can restore files from Trash or permanently delete them after 30 days.
- **Syncing**: The process of ensuring that the files on your local device are automatically updated with your files stored in Google Drive, keeping them consistent across platforms.
- Google Photos: A photo storage and sharing service that integrates with Google Drive. It allows you to back up and organize your photos and videos.2. Quick-Start Cheat Sheet

Quick Reference Guide

Here's a quick-reference guide that summarizes the essential steps and tips for getting started with Google Drive.

1. **Sign Up for Google Drive**:
   - o If you don't already have one, create a Google Account.
   - o Visit drive.google.com to access your Drive.
2. **Uploading Files**:

- o **Drag-and-Drop**: Simply drag files or folders into your Google Drive to upload them.
- o **Using the Menu**: Click on the "+ New" button and select either "File upload" or "Folder upload."

3. **Creating Folders**:
   - o Click the "+ New" button and select "Folder." Name your folder and click "Create."

4. **Creating and Editing Files**:
   - o **Google Docs/Sheets/Slides**: Click the "+ New" button, select the desired app (Docs, Sheets, or Slides), and start creating.
   - o **Offline Editing**: Enable offline mode by going to Settings > Offline and selecting files to be available offline.

5. **Sharing Files**:
   - o **Share via Link**: Right-click on a file/folder and select "Get link." Choose your sharing settings and send the link.
   - o **Share via Email**: Click the "Share" button, enter the recipient's email, and select their permission level.

6. **Syncing Files**:
   - o Download and install the Google Drive desktop app to sync files between your computer and Google Drive automatically.
   - o Customize which folders to sync via the app's preferences.

7. **Version History**:
   - o Right-click on any Google Doc, Sheet, or Slide file, select "Version History," and choose "See version history" to track changes and restore previous versions.

8. **Managing Storage**:
   o Review your storage by visiting Google Drive Storage.
   o Remove large or unnecessary files by right-clicking and selecting "Remove," then "Permanently delete" in Trash.

Google Drive Tips

- **Search**: Use the search bar to quickly locate files. You can filter by file type, owner, or modification date.
- **Offline Mode**: Set up offline access for essential files you may need when there's no internet connection. Go to the file, right-click, and select "Available offline."
- **Use Google Keep**: Create quick notes and lists in Google Keep, and easily link them to your Drive files for a comprehensive organizational system.
- **Organize Folders with Colors**: Use color-coding for your folders to visually differentiate between different types of documents.
- **Setting Up Notifications**: You can set up notifications to receive alerts when changes are made to shared documents. This is available in the "Notifications" section of Google Drive.

Index

Account Security, 90

Activity Dashboard, 52

Add-ons, 85

Advanced Search, 54

Archiving, 64

Cloud Storage, 2

Colors and Labels, 26

Desktop Interface, 16

Drag-and-Drop, 20

Email Invitations, 38

Email Notifications, 50

Expiration Dates, 42

File Privacy, 88

Filtering, 57

Freeing Up Space, 107

Google Account, 4

Google Drive's Free vs. Paid Storage Plans, 10

Google One, 10

Links, 36

means, *i*

Mobile App, 18

New Files, 30

Offline Access, 67

Offline Mode, 69, 98

Permission Levels, 39

Restoring Files, 65

Search Bar, 54

Search Operators, 56

Selective Sync, 68

Shared Drives, 80

Starred" Feature, 27

Sync Errors, 108

Syncing, 67

Tags or Descriptions, 60

Templates, 32

Two-Factor Authentication (2FA), 90

Update Google Drive, 109

Upload, 20

Version History, 48

Web Interface, 13